**Endo**

Gail illustrates so eloquent̲ ̲ ̲ ̲ ̲ ̲ ̲ ̲ ̲ ̲ ̲ ̲ ̲ in which we live and the desper̲ ̲ ̲ ̲ ̲ ̲ ̲ ̲ ̲ ̲ ̲ ̲ .aviui. Her story is one of truth, and it took courage to take a stand for decency in a land that has given itself over to the worldly, ruling spirit of this age. Written from personal experience and the pain and devastation brought by her own participation in this worldliness, she vividly portrays how her life was transformed when she turned herself over to the God who sent His son to die for us.

This book is a must read for anyone who has the courage to face the facts and raw truth about today's world. What is so refreshing is that woven into the fabric of this book is the story of redemption and its availability to all of us as His people. Gail is a modern day Jeremiah crying out to a lost and dying generation. Our prayer is that they will have ears to hear and eyes to see the prophetic words on these beautifully written pages.

Bobby & Dianne Lloyd
Long Island Citizens for Community Values
Protecting women, children, families and the community for 20 years!

Gail Koop is a gifted poet and author. Her sincere love for her Lord and Savior Jesus Christ is expressed through her writings. Her book, *Broken Land*, is a fine example of this. In her book, Gail humbly and honestly shares the story of how she experienced the powerful life-changing Grace of God. She writes about family, growing up in a secular Jewish home, struggles with alcoholism and immorality, being spiritually lost and finding faith in Jesus, her Messiah. But that's not all. Gail boldly explains how Holy Scripture both addresses the spiritual and moral decay of our present culture and proclaims its only hope can be found through Jesus Christ. Gail also weaves into her message many of her God-given prophetic dreams and poems, which prompted her to write the book. In summary, the same Jesus who healed Gail's broken life can heal our "broken land."

As Gail's pastor, I highly endorse her book. It is well written and Gail is a genuine Christian who "walks the talk." I have personally witnessed the life-changing Grace of God in Gail's life. I first talked to Gail 11 years ago when she phoned our church sincerely seeking God's purpose for her life. Happily, she found it. She was saved by God's Grace through faith and began a personal relationship with Jesus Christ. Gail is now a mature Christian serving in church leadership, and her heart's desire is to share with others the hope and truths she has found. This is why she wrote her book. May all who read it find the life-changing hope that only The Lord and Savior Jesus Christ can give!

Rev. Eric J. Rey
Pastor, Hampton Bays Assembly of God

Moses, the great Old Testament leader of Israel wrote, "I have set before you life and death, blessings and curses. Now choose life...that you may love the Lord your God, listen to His voice, and hold fast to Him" (Deuteronomy 30:19).

Our lives are primarily determined by our choices. A similar phrase that reverberates in my mind is "Decisions Determine Destiny." Occasionally, someone writes a book that exhorts us to bold choices. Such is the book you hold in your hand.

My friend, Gail Koop, courageously reveals many of the decisions she has made in her life—both the bad and good. She reveals them in an audacious, uninhibited, very non-politically-correct manner. This is not written to be sensational or shocking, but to let the reader in on the deep concerns of her heart.

Gail's concern is for the life and soul of humanity. She writes frankly of her past choices and their subsequent consequences. These experiences form the catalyst for her love that sounds the alarm to contemporary society—a society that is making far too many choices leading to narcissism, immorality, and meaninglessness.

Here's the good news. Gail is a dynamic disciple of Jesus Christ! Her redeemed soul and Biblical perspectives are God's gifts of grace to her. Her spiritual journey is woven throughout each chapter. That is the marrow of this book. May Gail's words not only challenge you, but above all, point you to the love-drenched Lord who graciously offers His forgiveness and eternal life! See John 3:16. Choose wisely, my friend.

Pastor Tim Rezac
Harvest Bible Chapel
Turks & Caicos Islands

Gail Koop has been a good friend of mine for quite a few years. I have found her to be a very humble and sincere person; one who is interested in blessing you in every way she can. That is why I know *Broken Land* has been written for the purpose of bringing to light some of the most predominant issues of our time, and to help us understand them better.

Sometimes, because we haven't had personal experience with certain situations or problems, we tend to either minimize or exaggerate their effects on ourselves and others. One of the things that Gail does through this book is to clarify the consequences of wrong thinking as it pertains to today's culture.

I am the survivor of a pregnancy that was almost aborted because my father wasn't ready to financially provide for me. Because of that, I highly value life and am very grateful to be living out the purpose of my existence. Gail uses her own life experiences to illuminate our hearts about the moral issues of our time.

My hope is that *Broken Land* will not be immediately rejected by those who have preconceived thoughts and ideas about the topics it addresses. It is important that we open our minds and hearts to wisdom that perhaps we've never heard, because in doing so, we may find the truth. And when we know the truth, it sets us free to stand for what we know is right, and it brings peace to our souls.

Christine Pickering
Director, New Wine Christian Women's Ministry

BROKEN LAND

God's Message in a Bottle

"Choose life so that you and your children will live..."
— Deuteronomy 30:19

Gail Koop

OlivePress צהר זית

Messianic & Christian Publisher

BROKEN LAND *God's Message in a Bottle*

ISBN: 978-1-941173-19-0

Published by
Olive Press Messianic and Christian Publisher
olivepresspublisher.com

Printed in the USA

Cover design by Cheryl Zehr
Cover photos copyright © 2016 by Shutterstock.com.
Photo on page 136 from www.phila.gov/districtattorney/pdfs/grandjurywomens-medical.pdf (page 102 of the pdf). Public record.

Gail Koop, author
gailfkoop@aol.com
www.framedbytheword.com

This book is dedicated to my husband, Jerry,
whose unwavering support is behind every word.

Table of Contents

Prologue: 1975

I was on the way to "end my pregnancy." At least that's how I thought of it at the time.

As I leaned forward to give the taxi driver the clinic's address, the safety pin holding my skirt together popped and stuck me in the side. I flinched at the momentary prick, unaware of the visceral pain I was to experience in about an hour.

Refastening the pin, I leaned back into the worn leather seat and a button on my blouse gave way. Although just ten weeks pregnant, my body had already begun preparing to nurture the life I was about to snuff out. Except back then, I didn't think it was a life.

It was 1975, just two years after the Roe vs. Wade decision made abortion legal. The ruling also established that what was inside of me was not a "person," convincing women in my situation—young, pregnant, unmarried—that a "fetus" or an "embryo" wasn't a baby. It was just a blob of tissue that could be eradicated by a surgical procedure that would take about twenty minutes and cost about two hundred dollars. But if what was inside of me wasn't living, why had my body changed so much?

The driver pulled up to the walkway of the brick building. I don't remember its name, but it was something innocuous like, "Women's Medical Center." I paid and tipped the driver, then reached into my purse to make sure the wad of twenty-dollar bills given to me by a friend the day before was easily accessible.

I checked in with the receptionist, who sat behind a glass partition. A clipboard was on the counter in front of her, which she began eyeing to find my name. I spotted it before she did, even though I was reading upside down. I had become adept at viewing things upside down, which is why I didn't think I was about to do anything wrong. I removed the bills from my purse and slid them through the small opening in the glass above the counter. Payment was required up front.

A woman in a white smock, who I assumed was a nurse, escorted me into a small, windowless room. It had an armless chair, a stool with a pile of neatly folded gowns, and a steel table with stirrups, just like what you'd find in any gynecologist's office. She told me to undress from the waist down, put on one of the gowns, and then to sit on the table and wait for the doctor. She said she'd be returning with him in a few minutes.

She left the room and I did what she said. As I sat on the table, the cold steel sent a shivering thought into my mind: *was I doing the right thing?* Even though I had been convinced that there was no other choice, when the door opened, the thought echoed. A masked doctor, accompanied by the nurse, now also wearing a mask, wheeled in a machine and positioned it next to my left leg.

The nurse instructed me to lie back and place my feet in the stirrups, which I did. After the doctor plugged in the machine, he stood between my splayed legs and told me what was going to happen. In a very business-like manner, he said that he was going to insert a speculum into my vagina, just like when I'm having a pap smear, and inject something to help numb the area. Then he would insert a plastic tube, which was attached to the machine, which would enable the procedure. He also told me that once the procedure started I would feel something like menstrual cramps. What he didn't tell me was that the tube had a knife-like tip that would shred the baby inside of me to pieces, which would be suctioned through the tube into a bottle that would be thrown away.

I heard the click of a switch, then a roaring noise. As the nurse took my hand, I felt the tube snake its way to my womb. And then the siege began. My insides were torn apart, tugged and pulled in every direction as the whir of the machine drowned out my cries. And it didn't feel like menstrual cramps at all. Those happen when a woman's body sheds material that has naturally built up during the month to prepare for a pregnancy that didn't happen. What was occurring here was the dismembering of the child that had attached itself, as it was meant to, to that material. The pain was unlike any I had ever experienced. Then again, I had never had a part of my body removed before.

On the taxi ride back to my apartment, I felt no relief, no gleeful anticipation of my clothes fitting once again. What I did feel was an unexplained sadness over the thick pad and warm flow between my legs. When I got home, I fell onto my platform bed crying, feeling so alone, so remorseful. Even with all the pro-abortion indoctrination and cultural excitement over the newly won Roe vs. Wade decision, in my heart I knew I had done something very wrong.

But how did I know that? And why? What I had just done was not only legal; it was encouraged, even celebrated. What I didn't understand then was that just because something is legal, just because it is encouraged or celebrated, doesn't mean that it is moral. And even though, at twenty-four, I didn't know the Moral Giver, there was something deep within me that echoed His "yes and no, right and wrong..." (Romans 2:15). Yet, like footprints washed by the tide, that horrific experience would become a grainy memory. And I would once again find myself on another cold steel table.

Why do we do that? Why do we innately know right from wrong, yet continue to do wrong? And what will happen if we don't stop?

It took decades of doing the wrong things before I found the answers to those questions. And I'm grateful to be able to share them with you through the pages that follow.

4

Then and Now

That was me--
High heels, tight dress,
Corporate climbing
With all the rest.

Sunglassed, smoking,
Strutting Madison,
Lunching on Sabretts,
Trysting at the Radisson.

Ann Taylor suits,
Corner office, walnut desk,
My god my boss--
Who would have guessed

A freight train of time
Would flatten it all,
Or three decades later
Those memories would pall

At the now of You
And the now of me,
At who You are
And who, in You, I can be.

Introduction

"This is a trustworthy saying, and everyone should accept it: 'Christ Jesus came into the world to save sinners'—and I am the worst of them all. But God had mercy on me so that Christ Jesus could use me as a prime example of his great patience with even the worst sinners. Then others will realize that they, too, can believe in him and receive eternal life" (1 Timothy 1: 15-16 NLT).

Picture someone prostrate on the floor. That was my spiritual position as I wrote this book.

In addition to having had two abortions, I've used drugs and struggled with alcoholism all of my adult life. I've even woken up with strange men in my bed because I was too drunk the night before to care. So moral apostasy is the last thing I ever dreamed I'd write about.

But when I was several chapters into a memoir (about how a secular Jewish girl became a born-again Christian), I was abruptly redirected by just that—a dream.

I'm now in my sixties, and I've been dreaming all my life. Many people say they don't remember their dreams, but I always have. They've been like movies, clear and entertaining. In fact, there was a rent-poor time in my twenties when I looked forward to going to sleep because I couldn't afford to go to the movies.

From the time I was a young girl I've loved to write, and have kept journals on and off throughout my life. But I didn't begin journaling my dreams on a regular basis until I became a Christian at 53. Before that, my dreams were wild and crazy, as most are, with the usual scenarios of flying, being chased, or appearing in public nude or scantily clad. But after I had completely surrendered my heart to Jesus Christ, my dreams began to change.

I started to dream about and have visions of Scripture references. I dreamed about things and situations in people's lives that subsequently happened. And I had dreams that began to reflect the moral decay in our culture. Only I didn't realize that's what they were about, until the dream that birthed this book.

It was a dream that removed any doubt as to whether God was speaking, a dream that revealed what Jesus meant when He said to His disciples, "Whoever wants to be my disciple must deny themselves and take up their cross and follow me" (Matthew 16:24 TNIV). Because this book, and the message it contains, is my cross.

But before I tell you about that dream, it's important for you to know what led up to it, as well as a little about me, so that hopefully and prayerfully you will see that it is God's Spirit, not mine, directing this. What follows is "about me" only in that sense.

 Part One

About Me

"It's not about you."

The purpose of your life is far greater than your own personal fulfillment, your peace of mind, or even your happiness. It's far greater than your family, your career, or even your wildest dreams and ambitions. If you want to know why you were placed on this planet, you must begin with God. You were born *by* his purpose and *for* his purpose.

—Rick Warren
The Purpose Driven Life[1]

Roots

I am of all
That went before,
Not just the seed
My mother bore.

I am of psalmists,
Prophets and kings,
Of a land that groans
To once again sing.

I am of DNA
So skillfully carved
Fifty years of drought
Have left me starved

For the living water
From which I came,
For whom I now thirst—
The Name above all names.

I am of Christ,
A person anew,
Seeded in salvation—
Forever a Jew.

Chapter One
Discovering My Roots

"He made peace between Jews and Gentiles by creating in himself one new people from the two groups" (Ephesians 2:15 NLT).

In the natural world, who we become is defined by genetics and life experiences, particularly those from childhood. As we age we tend to see in ourselves the very traits we disliked in our parents, and sometimes live out our lives trying to change or overcome them. But once God gets hold of us, as He did with me, we come to understand that the particular sperm and egg that came together to create us was part of a preordained plan. "For you created my inmost being; you knit me together in my mother's womb...My frame was not hidden from you when I was made in the secret place...All the days ordained for me were written in your book before one of them came to be" (Psalm 139:13, 15-16).

My father, David Fishgold, was a second-generation Russian Jew. As a child, the only time I remember him using the name of Jesus Christ was when he was mad or frustrated. He'd often say he didn't believe in organized religion, referring to that, as Karl Marx did, as "an opiate for the people." He believed that religion was an ideological tool used to legitimize and defend the interests of the upper classes. I suppose today his worldview would be called "secular progressive," maybe even socialist.

My dad called himself a "Deist," explaining that he believed there was a God who created everything, but that He wasn't involved in our every day lives. Although this left me with a confused picture of a disengaged God up in the sky just watching everything, it did at least leave me with a belief that there *was* a God.

My mother, Susie Owanna Kimbrough, was a Scotch-Irish farm girl who had a Bible-believing mother. Although my mom never spoke about God, and I can't remember ever seeing a Bible in our house, one summer she did send my younger sister and I to a vacation Bible school. Only God knew that the song planted in my heart that summer would, half a century later, become life transforming. "Jesus loves me, this I know, for the Bible tells me so."

At Christmas time, we'd have a Charlie Brown tree, an electrified plastic menorah in the kitchen window, and multicolored lights strung along the roof gutter. Though I knew we had the mishmash of symbols to represent Christmas and Hanukkah because of my parents' backgrounds, we never went to church or temple.

I grew up in Levittown, a small town on Long Island in New York. I was the middle of five children, and had an older brother and sister and a younger brother and sister. Most families in our neighborhood (including my two best girlfriends) were Catholic, so being Jewish was an anomaly. Beyond staying home from school on Jewish holidays and opening a bottle of Manischewitz on my brothers' thirteenth birthdays, our heritage was never explained. So as I watched my friends go to church and catechism each week, I began to feel left out, different. One of my friend's fathers used to repeatedly say to me, "A nice girl like you ought to be a Catholic." Of course that made me feel even more different, and that there was something wrong with being Jewish.

Occasionally, I'd go to church with that family. I remember sitting in the pew of the cavernous sanctuary, rainbows of light streaming through stained glass depictions of people and scenes I didn't understand. And I clearly recall two emotions that now make sense to me. One was a sense of awe at the fact that this was where God was supposed to be. The other was that when the priest spoke, though I didn't understand what he said, I had a deep desire to.

Once when I was in middle school and my dad was reading the paper, I told him that I didn't "feel" Jewish.

He lowered the newspaper beneath his chin and locked his brown eyes with mine. "Oh yeah?" An unlit stogie danced in the corner of his mouth. "Well what's your last name?"

"Fishgold," I said.

As if some major point had been made, he flicked the paper, straightening it between his hands and lifted it up again, covering his face. "You're Jewish." And that was that. For him, anyway. But it wouldn't be until some forty years later when I would walk into a small Christian church (Chapter Three explains why) that I would actually start to "feel" Jewish.

During my first weeks attending that church, my pastor found out that my father was Jewish. And he beamed, "Oh! So you're a Messianic Jew!" Seeing the confused look on my face he explained. "That means that you're a Jew who believes that Jesus is the Messiah." It was then that the Charlie Brown tree and plastic menorah began to make sense. Because to my surprise, I began to discover that Christianity is rooted in Judaism: Jesus, His disciples, and the first church were all Jewish.

The same year I walked into that church was the year my father's oldest sister, my Aunt Betty, passed away at the age of 95. My dad had passed away about six years earlier. Unbeknownst to any of us, my aunt had written a memoir, which a friend published a few months after my aunt's passing. It documents stories about our ancestry that were told to her by my grandfather. Through that book, I discovered just how deep my Jewish roots go.

Five generations of my father's family came from a small town in Ukraine, Russia called Talne. The town was comprised primarily of orthodox Russian Jews.

My grandfather, Samuel, studied the Talmud and his brother, Charlie, studied to be a Rabbi until he was drafted into the Russian army. I had great aunts and uncles with names like Miriam, Bathsheba, Yenta, and Moishe. My great grandfather, Sholom, prayed at home three times a day. My aunt describes him "wearing a long white prayer shawl and a Tefillin, which consisted of black leather straps which he wound around his arm, and wore a little black box on his forehead. He wore his yarmulke constantly indoors and under his hat outdoors."

When my grandfather was seventeen, my great grandparents were almost killed in a pogrom in the late 1800s. Pogroms were violent riots led by the Cossacks, an orthodox Catholic Russian military group bent on persecuting and committing massacres against Jewish people.

My aunt tells of my grandfather being told on the way home from school, "'Quick, run home. The Cossacks are murdering your father and mother!'" She wrote that he "started running, picking up a large piece of wood, like a club, on the way. He found his parents on the floor, bloodied, but alive. Apparently he gained supernatural strength, and managed to swing that club with such strength it debilitated the attackers, and they retreated. Although they were never attacked again, from that moment on, they lived in fear." A few years later, at the age of 21, my grandfather immigrated to the United States.

My grandfather died when I was a child. I have a few vague memories of him. One is when he'd take me to a nearby park and push me on a swing. Another is sitting on his lap at home while he sang Yiddish songs and bounced me on his knees.

My mother's parents were southern migrant farmers who picked cotton for a living. When they were eventually able to buy their own small farm in Arkansas, my mother said she and her brothers and sister (also five siblings), when they weren't in school, had to work in the fields with sacks on their backs, picking cotton in the hot sun. She said she always wished for rain, because then they wouldn't have to work and could play in the barn in the hay.

My maternal grandfather, Webster, was a twin whose brother died in childbirth. So, because twins tend to run in families and sometimes skip generations, I always expected one of my siblings or I to have twins. But no one did. I've had dreams involving twins, both babies and grown children. Although I know I'm forgiven, the thought that I could have aborted twins now breaks my heart. But it has also helped propel me to write this book.

My maternal grandmother, Florence, was a petite, quiet woman who, according to my mother, regularly read her Bible. Until I applied for a passport and had to get a copy of my birth certificate, I never knew that I was named after her. My given name is officially recorded as "Florence Fishgold." When I asked my mother about it, she said my father didn't like the name Florence, so he changed it to Gail.

My mom also told me that my grandmother had what used to be called, "second sight," that she had dreams and visions that came to pass. One was about her son, my Uncle Johnny, that he appeared at the foot of her bed while he was overseas in the army. Dressed in his uniform, he told her that he'd been wounded, but that he was going to be all right. A few days later, two officers came to the house and delivered that exact message. My grandmother had a weak heart and told my mother if it weren't for that dream, she might have had a heart attack at the sight of those soldiers at her door.

The stories about my maternal grandmother and paternal grandfather make so much sense to me now. Not only am I my grandmother's namesake, but God has blessed me with her gift of prophetic dreaming. And my ancestral Jewish roots have drawn me to the Old Testament, to the prophets and their warnings. So much of what God has put on my heart for this book, so much of what He has revealed through dreams and confirmed through His Word, the Bible, echoes what He spoke thousands of years ago to the nation of Israel, the Jewish people.

And those ancient words and warnings still apply to us today—and will apply to every generation yet to come—because God "is the same yesterday, today, and forever" (Hebrews 13:8 NKJV). We may look different than people of Biblical times, but the human heart has not changed. "The LORD does not look at the things human beings look at. People look at the outward appearance, but the LORD looks at the heart" (1 Samuel 16:7 TNIV).

Before I walked into that Christian church, I was one of those "people" to whom outward appearances mattered so much. I wanted my parents to look different, act different, to be more like my girlfriends' parents, more like the ones on the *Father Knows Best* and *Donna Reed* TV shows. I was embarrassed for anyone to come to our house because it was always a chaotic mess. And when a friend did come over, I can still feel the knot in my stomach if they asked to use the bathroom. We couldn't afford to have our cesspool pumped, so the toilet would often overflow.

But looking back, it's as if I've been given an anointed pair of binoculars. I can now focus in and see how genetics and experiences have played a part in the person I've become. More importantly, though, because the love of God has been so mercifully shed abroad in my heart (Romans 5:5), I can now see my parents through the unconditionally loving eyes of God.

Chapter Two
Understanding My Parents

"Honor your father and your mother..." (Exodus 20:12).

"As long as you've got your health, a roof over your head, clothes on your back, food on the table and a family who loves you, you've got everything." That was my father's annoying response whenever I'd ask for something that we didn't have or couldn't afford.

Now, using those anointed binoculars, I see the Christ-like wisdom in those words. It's very similar to what Paul told Timothy, "So if we have enough food and clothing, let us be content" (1 Timothy 6:8 NLT). But as a child all I could see was what my girlfriends had—newer cars, designer clothes, and nicer houses with toilets that always flushed. And even though I loved my father, I also secretly wished he were different, too.

While my girlfriends' fathers were businessmen or tradesmen, my father was a presser, a "piece worker," who ironed dresses in a factory. I remember watching him get ready for work, sitting on a hassock in his boxer shorts, wrapping ace bandages from his ankles to his knees and securing them with silver clips that had teeth-like grips. He had bad varicose veins and his job required him to stand on his feet all day.

While my girlfriends' fathers earned steady paychecks, my father got paid according to the number of dresses he pressed—at five cents a dress. One summer when I was about eleven, my dad took me to work with him. It was there that I was introduced to a "sweatshop."

The factory was cavernous and without air conditioning. The ceiling seemed at least twenty feet high and had scores of irons, strung on long poles, hanging from it. Beneath each iron, creating separate workspaces, were two tables and a clothes rack with hangers. One table was shaped like an ironing board and the other was piled high with dresses. A good portion of the factory was filled with women busily sewing on machines, making the dresses for my father and the other men to press.

Seeing my father work was like watching a movie in fast-forward. My dad stood over his ironing table, a towel around his neck to catch and wipe the sweat, and slid dress after dress over the mouth of the table, turning, pressing, turning pressing. I was astounded by the speed at which he moved. My job that day was to hang each dress up as he finished. But he was so fast that I hadn't even hung one dress before he handed me the next. I'll never hear the steamy hiss of an iron without thinking of my dad wiping the sweat from his face on that August day in New York City.

At five cents a dress, I can only imagine the mental calculator as he thought of his wife, five children, mortgage, and bills. To make one hundred dollars, he had to press two thousand dresses a week, or four hundred a day. Unbelievably, that's a dress a minute. And he did that for at least eight hours a day, five days a week. And on weekends, he worked in a diner as a short order cook.

But amazingly, either before he left for work or after he got home, my father always made time for us. He was the one who read us bedtime stories and tucked us in at night. He was the one who asked about school and helped with our homework. But his love, at times, felt suffocating.

When he was home, my dad would hover over us, afraid to let us out of his sight. We weren't allowed to lock our bedroom doors because he was always afraid of a fire. He even made us have fire drills on Sunday mornings, where we'd have to tie sheets to a bedpost and then throw them out of the second story window. All I could think of was the neighbors passing by, laughing at the Jewish presser's family.

But again, through my aunt's memoir, I came to understand why my father was so over protective. My grandmother died when my father was two years old. My grandfather couldn't care for all of their five children by himself, so he had to temporarily put my dad and his brothers and sisters in an orphanage. They also spent some years with foster families before my grandfather remarried and could take them home. My father was afraid of losing us, the way he lost his home and parents.

My mother always seemed to be in the background, allowing my father to take the lead emotionally. She was busy either taking care of us, lying down reading, or making a meal. It wasn't until after she died that I came to understand that while my dad loved us loudly, my mom loved us silently.

My mother was born in Neshoba, Mississippi. She met my father at a USO club in Texas, where she was a waitress. She was nineteen and he was a thirty-year-old, movie-star-handsome soldier. He swept her off her feet—literally. She was still nineteen and pregnant with my sister when they got married.

My mom gave birth to my sister, Betty, in Abilene, Texas and then stayed with her parents on their Arkansas farm while my father was overseas. When he returned on leave, he whisked her and Betty up north to Brooklyn, where his family was. They were a tight knit group, again, because of their upbringing and my mother never did acclimate, either to them or to city life. By the time we moved to Levittown in 1956, my mother had had four children: Betty, Irving (named after my father's half brother who was killed in the Spanish Civil War), me, and April. John, the youngest, would be born in Levittown.

You can take the girl out of the country, but you can't take the country out of the girl. Up until the end of her life, this describes my mother. She was never able to reconcile herself to the north, always secretly longing for the people, mountains, and the music of the Ozarks. Maybe that unfulfilled longing contributed to her inability to demonstrably show her love to us. It wasn't until she became older and perhaps more aware of her mortality, that when my sisters or I would tell her we loved her, she began to respond, "Love you more."

After my mother died at the age of 91, my sisters and I went through her things. We were surprised to find that she was a prolific poet. And it was through the words she was never able to speak out loud that we discovered how much our mother loved us. Here are some excerpts:

> I knew a brief time of happiness
> But it was not mine to keep
> When I held my babies to my heart
> And rocked them gently and sweetly to sleep
> I was content when they needed me
> But then they were gone
> Now here I am again
> Unhappy and alone
> ***
> My daughters were a treasure
> God put within my keeping
> For just a few short years
> That ended with silent weeping

My father would have liked nothing better than for all of us to live in that Levitt house with him forever. He was so upset when my sisters and I moved out to start our own lives that he wouldn't speak to us for months afterward. My mother, as usual, was silent on the issue. Until her words spoke to us after her passing.

> Because my love for you can let you go
> It doesn't mean I love you less
> It means I understand your need
> And only want your happiness

In another poem, entitled, "To My Children," my mother asked us not to bury her, but to:

> ...Let the cleansing fire destroy this shell
> Where my soul and spirit too long did dwell
> Then take my ashes to Mountain View
> The place I love, as I've often told you.
> Climb a mountain that's high and quiet
> It doesn't matter if it's day or night
> Scatter my ashes into the wind
> And say a prayer as they descend...

One year after my mother's memorial service, my sisters, two cousins, and I did just that. We rented a cabin in Mountain View, Arkansas for three days and explored the place that had held my mother's heart. As we walked through the streets of the town, heard the folk music played in the square and met and talked with the local people, I finally understood who my mother was: a simple country girl.

In Matthew 7:1, Jesus tells us not to judge, or we will be judged. Yet, because I didn't know Jesus Christ and therefore had no idea what the Truth really was, I spent a lifetime judging my mother, wanting her to be different, wanting her to be like "other mothers."

It is only through the grace of God that I am now able to understand and truly love who my mother and father were. I am so grateful for the Lord's perspective on who we all are: "for all have sinned and fall short of the glory of God" (Romans 3:23). We are people who fall short every day, imperfect people who need a Savior. My father walked through his life not knowing who that Savior is. I believe that, in God's unfathomable mercy, He revealed Himself to my dad in his final hour. And that my father took His hand.

My mom knew Jesus Christ as her Lord and Savior, but she continually said that she never felt worthy. No matter how I tried to convince her that none of us are, I don't think she truly realized that until the very end. She died in the arms of my sister and niece. And they said that at the last minute, right before she took her last breath, she opened her eyes wide as saucers. They said there was a look of amazement on her face, as if she was seeing something awesome. I believe it was some form of Heaven, or someone who had come to take her there. Maybe she saw her mother. Maybe she saw Jesus Himself. Or maybe she saw her son, my brother, Irving—the unlikely person who led me to the Savior who transformed me from the inside out.

The Wonder of God

Like the lion
In the Wizard of Oz,
I was a coward
When it came to God.

Afraid to surrender
Myself to that might,
Afraid to expose
My heart to the light.

So I "new-aged" my mind,
Let those thoughts guide my path,
While secretly dreading
The storm of God's wrath.

But what happened instead
Was a huge surprise,
When God found me
Through my dying brother's eyes.

Which shone not with anger
But with a loving reprieve,
As I echoed the cowardly lion:
I do believe, I do believe.

Chapter Three
Transforming My Mind

"Do not conform any longer to the pattern of this world, but be transformed by the renewing of your mind. Then you will be able to test and approve what God's will is – his good, pleasing and perfect will" (Romans 12:2 NIV).

At the time of this writing, it was just ten years ago that I was one of the biggest conformists "to the pattern of this world." It's how I wound up with two unwanted pregnancies, and why I ended them through abortion. It's how I became an alcoholic. It's why I led such a promiscuous life.

But my perspective began to shift when God found me through the circumstances surrounding my brother's death.

My Conversion

"How can a man be born when he is old?" (John 3:4 NKJV).

My older brother, Irving, struggled with mental illness ever since he was a teenager. On the advice of doctors and psychologists, my mom and dad reluctantly agreed to hospitalize him the summer he turned seventeen. It was a horrible time for our family. I was thirteen.

He was released at the end of that summer, just before school, and for a time did well. I remember how happy

I was, and how freeing and normal it felt to ride on the handlebars of my big brother's bicycle. And my heart still pangs at his sweet awkwardness when he let me give him a few dance lessons. But by the fall, Irving was unable to stay in school. His doctor felt that the army would provide a good structure for him. So my parents signed the papers allowing him to enlist.

And it turned out the doctors were right. In the army, Irving received his GED and learned his craft as an airplane mechanic. While he was stationed in Germany, he met and married my sister-in-law and subsequently had four children. Sadly, they lost their third child, Joshua, born three months premature with an undeveloped heart and lungs that couldn't sustain him.

Even though Irving was able to maintain himself in the army, learn a trade, marry and have a family, he still wasn't emotionally stable. But because he would never admit to having a problem, he wasn't willing to take medication. As a result, he estranged many of the people who loved him the most, including me.

Irving's untreated mental illness eventually convinced him that I was the reason for every bad thing that had ever happened to him. When he was 57 and I was 53, Irving was diagnosed with esophageal cancer and wasn't expected to recover. At that time, we had been estranged for about seven years, during which he'd had several heart attacks. Each time I would reach out to him. But each time he would hurl accusations that would slam my heart like a shot-put, and another period of silence would ensue. With this latest diagnosis, however, I knew I needed to see him, even though my fear was practically crippling. So I got on my knees and prayed to a god I did not know, that Irving would realize how much I loved him before he died.

When my sisters decided to visit Irving in the hospital, even though he strongly objected to seeing any of us, I decided to join them. Irving had developed a lung infection, was quarantined, and all visitors were required to wear surgical masks. As we entered his room, I felt suffocated not only by the difficulty of breathing beneath the stiff fabric, but by the familiar tightening in my chest as any thought of my brother had come to evoke.

The shrunken person wearing an oxygen mask and sitting on the edge of the bed was a caricature of the burly six-foot man I remembered. Just as I dreaded, he targeted me like a heat-seeking missile, locking eyes with mine. As oxygen-fed accusations squeaked at me beneath his mask, all I could manage beneath mine was a muffled, "Irving, I love you."

He immediately quieted and looked at me, wide-eyed, like a child. And magnified behind the lenses of his glasses, I witnessed the demons drown in the clear, blue-green Mediterranean of his eyes. In a moment that will always be in the present tense, he said, "I love you, too, Gail. I've always loved you. Sometimes I just didn't know how to act. So I'd lash out. I'm sorry if I ever hurt you. I never meant to." And he held out his hand to me. I took it in both of mine, then reached around his bony shoulders and hugged my brother for the first time in seven years. My sisters then took their turns.

For the next three days, before he was placed on a respirator, I had my brother back. The brother who rode me on the handlebars of his bicycle that summer, as the smell of grass on the wind branded the memory. The brother I taught how to dance, our socks catching on the attic's plywood floor as "The Bristol Stomp" spun on the portable record player.

Irving had been on a respirator for almost three weeks when my sister-in-law, a born again Christian, called in a Messianic rabbi (a rabbi who believes Jesus is the Messiah). After years of sarcastic, antagonistic criticism of his wife's faith, through a nod of his head and with tears streaming down his cheeks, my brother acknowledged Yeshua, the Hebrew name for Jesus, as Lord of his life. Irving died the next day. And the rage-filled pain was visceral. I felt teased, cheated. Why was he given back, only to be taken away?

Miraculously, the answer came from my brother. When my niece was going through Irving's study, she found some copied pages from Charles Stanley's book, *The Blessings of Brokenness* on his desk. These passages were highlighted, as if by the sun:

> God will break and keep on breaking us
> until all resentment, hostility, anger and
> self importance have been broken out of

our lives.... Often as people struggle with
terminal disease, the outer body literally
seems to waste away, yet if they are willing
to turn to God and to submit completely
to Him and trust Him with their lives, the
inner beauty and spiritual strength begins
to develop that far out shadows and far
outweighs anything happening in the
physical realm. [2]

And the plates of the earth shifted inside me. Rage
became gratitude. And doubt became a hunger to find
the God who had not only so specifically answered my
prayer—that Irving would know that I loved him—but had
given me an even greater gift: a profession of my brother's
love for me. Even if it only lasted three days, it was so
much more than I could ever have asked or imagined
(Ephesians 3:20).

I knew that a lifetime of untreated mental illness
doesn't just disappear on its own. So I earnestly sought
out the Giver of that miraculous gift.

*"You will seek me and find me when you seek me with all
your heart"* (Jeremiah 29:13).

I had picked up *The Purpose Driven Life* by Rick
Warren a year before my brother died. The subtitle
intrigued me: *What on earth am I here for?* After Irving's
death, I remembered it and sought it out. I had never read
a word of Scripture before, but the words cut deep. Just
like it says in Hebrews 4:12 (NIV), "For the word of God is
living and active. Sharper than any double-edged sword,

it penetrates even to dividing soul and spirit, joints and marrow; it judges the thoughts and attitudes of the heart." I didn't know it at the time, of course, but the words were doing exactly what that verse describes.

As I read, I was amazed that the Bible had so much relevance to life, especially to my life. I literally could not put Pastor Warren's book down. When I finished, I was hungry for more, the way I used to want to read the next novel by my favorite authors. At the end of the book, Mr. Warren suggests finding a Bible-believing church. So the day I finished the book, I looked in my local town paper. Under "Churches and Temples," there was a tiny ad that said, "Spiritual Discussion: 40 Days of Purpose," with the name and phone number of a local church. Although Biblically significant, the number 40 meant nothing to me at the time, so I never made the connection with Pastor Warren's book, which talks about taking a 40-day journey.

When I called the church and asked the pastor what the "spiritual discussion" was about, he proceeded to describe everything I had just read. I asked him if this had anything to do with Rick Warren's book. He said yes, that they were beginning the DVD study of that very book. Incredulous, I told him that I had just finished the book that day and was hungry for more. He laughed and said, "Well, it certainly looks like God is working in your life!" (And only God knew how miraculously prophetic those words would prove to be. Nine years later I was elected to serve beside that pastor as Deaconess on the Church Council where I still serve today.)

Once I began going to church, the sermons weren't enough. I went to Bible studies and read everything I could get my hands on that spoke about Jesus. Because if He was God, as He claimed, then I wanted to know Him.

Some of the books I read were written by former atheists who had been won over by the irrefutable evidence of the resurrection and the twelve ordinary men who died martyrs deaths because of it. I couldn't understand how someone could be raised from the dead, but I couldn't find any proof that it didn't happen. And, as passionately as some want to disprove it, they have been unsuccessful for more than two thousand years.

Although I had trouble with the exclusivity of Jesus' statement that He was the only way, not one of many, I came to believe that Jesus was/is, in fact, God. And after that, whether or not I agreed with what He said or what the Bible said, my attitude was: who am I to argue with God?

And once I took that proverbial leap of faith, things began to change.

Sacred Ground

Fill me with Your purpose,
Shake me from this slumber.
Help my deceitful heart
Receive Your truth, Your wonder.

Scorn my pride, self-righteousness,
Show me who You are.
Bow me with humility
Beneath Your moon and stars.

Lift me from humanity,
Peel away this flesh.
Clothe me in Your Spirit,
Let Your yoke upon me rest.

Lead me on this journey
Where life and love abound.
Help me bear my cross
Above Your sacred ground.

Chapter Four
Processing the Messages

"For God speaks again and again, though people do not recognize it. He speaks in dreams, in visions of the night, when deep sleep falls on people as they lie in their beds" (Job 33:14-17 NLT).

As I mentioned in the Introduction, I've been dreaming all my life. But shortly after becoming a Christian, my dreams started to change. The first one had a brick wall with writing on it. But it wasn't the typical red brick and mortar wall. The bricks were shades of yellow and tan, they were large and rectangular and laid horizontally. Etched into the wall was "Jeremiah 15."

At the time I had no idea what that was or meant, other than Jeremiah was a book in the Old Testament. I picked up my new Bible (NLT) and found the writings of the Old Testament prophet. First, I went to Chapter 15 and began reading about Judah's doom. I understood very little, the apocalyptic prose scaring me. Then I turned to Jeremiah 1:5 and read, "I knew you before I formed you in your mother's womb. Before you were born I set you apart and appointed you as my spokesman to the world." Then I read further, verses 6 - 8. "'O Sovereign Lord...I can't speak for you! I'm too young!' 'Don't say that,' the Lord replied, 'for you must go wherever I send you and say whatever I tell you. And don't be afraid of the people, for I will be with you and take care of you. I, the LORD, have spoken!'" Though the vision from my dream was clear, what I was reading was so bizarre, I completely dismissed it.

About a year and a half later I felt a prompting, seemingly out of nowhere, to Google "The Western Wall." When I did, my jaw dropped. It was the "brick" wall in my dream. Same colors, same shaped stones. My heart raced as I printed the picture, then took a pen and wrote, "Jeremiah 15" across the bricks. It was the exact vision in my dream. But it was still unbelievable to me. My response this time, both out loud and in my heart was, "Oh. My. God." It was just too weird for me to at any level consider. I folded up the picture and slid it into one of the cubbies on my desk.

About a year after that, as I was driving home from a college visit with my daughter, an overwhelming impression came over me. It had to do with teaching or preaching. But in a huge way. The impression was so powerful I started to cry and almost pulled over. I audibly asked, "Lord, what is this? How can this be? I'm terrified of public speaking, and I'm totally unqualified to do what I feel You are telling me." I didn't know it then, but I was paraphrasing Moses. "O Lord, I have never been eloquent, neither in the past nor since you have spoken to your servant. I am slow of speech and tongue" (Exodus 4:10). I added, "If this is from You, I'm going to need major confirmation."

It was a six-hour drive, so I'd brought along recordings of several sermons from my church that I'd missed.

Wiping my eyes, I randomly grabbed a cassette (we hadn't yet upgraded to CDs) and slid it into the portable player on the passenger seat. My pastor began to speak. "Today we're going to talk about the apostles. Twelve ordinary men who God chose to do extraordinary work. We're going to see how God chooses and equips ordinary people for the most extraordinary tasks." Again, without me realizing it, the Lord was saying "...I will help you speak and will teach you what to say" (Exodus 4:12). As I sped down the parkway, disbelief strapped itself into the seat beside me.

In the days that followed, I couldn't get any of this out of my mind. I really did feel that God was speaking to me, but at the same time there were many roadblocks that kept me from believing it. One was that I was a woman, and most of the Biblical teaching I had experienced in my short time as a Christian was done by men. But one day when I was lying on the couch thinking about all of this, another Scripture reference came to mind. And remember, at the time I had no clue about any Scriptures at all. (My pastor had to give me those pre-printed dividers so that I could find books easier.) The Scripture reference was Philippians 4:3. When I looked it up, once again I was stunned. "Yes, and I ask you loyal yokefellow, help these women who have contended at my side in the cause of the gospel...."

For the next couple of years I had no desire to read a novel, and I hardly read a newspaper. I just devoured the Bible, craving only Biblical instruction and worship. During that time, I had many dreams about people and situations that eventually came to pass.

In one dream my sister was extremely tired and had Frankenstein-like stitches on the right side of her forehead. I called her the morning after I had the dream and told her about it. She said she had been very tired, and there had been a steady ache on the right side of her head. Three months later she was diagnosed with a nonmalignant tumor on the right frontal lobe of her brain. After her surgery, the stitches were in the exact spot as in the dream.

In another dream my pastor was in the hospital. Two months later, he had emergency gall bladder surgery. Another was about a friend, that something terrible had happened and she was in the hospital. A few days later I learned that her granddaughter had been born three months prematurely and my friend had been at the hospital the night I had the dream. There are many, many more.

I now believe that God used those and other dreams and their subsequent manifestations to convince me that He was speaking. But I didn't understand why, until the dream that birthed this book.

Chapter Five
Accepting the Assignment

"Then confront them with their detestable practices" (Ezekiel 23:36).

On March 3, 2011, I had a dream that a baby was handed to me. It was a girl, less than a year old. Her eyes were at half-mast, closing on and off, as if she'd been sleeping before she was given to me. She was wearing a pink and white striped "onesie," those one-piece tee shirts that snap around the baby's diaper. I held her very carefully in my arms, trying to determine the best way to hold her. Then I gently placed her on my shoulder.

Suddenly she was gone. And I knew she'd been put in a bottle and thrown in the trash in Brooklyn. I was in a panic and got in my car, heading to Brooklyn to try and find her. My thoughts were, *Could she breathe? Had the garbage truck come yet? Would the baby still be there?* It was, like so many of my dreams, weird. A baby in a bottle thrown in the trash? I recorded the dream in my journal, prayed a little about it, and came to the conclusion that the baby represented the "ministry" of sharing my faith, and that people were just throwing the Gospel message away.

A few months later the dream came to mind, with a prompting to Google "abortion and bottle." I was so taken aback by the out-of-the-blue thought, I didn't even think about my own abortions. But when I did the search, the world fell away. The procedure used in 80% of abortions is to suck the fetus into a bottle. The bottles are considered medical waste and disposed of as such. A baby in a bottle thrown in the trash. Again, Oh. My. God. But what about Brooklyn? So I did some more Googling and found that besides there being several medical waste sites in that borough of New York City, the word "Brooklyn" is derived from the Dutch language. Its original meaning is "Broken Land."

This was the point when I knew, without a doubt, that the dream had been about abortion, that God sees it as throwing life away, and that our land has become broken. And I was gripped with what I can only describe as utter panic when I also knew that it was the message I was supposed to write about.

I got on my knees and asked God why He hadn't revealed the true meaning of the dream at the time I had it. And what I heard in my heart devastated me. It was, *"Because you didn't ask Me."* And in hindsight, I hadn't. I thought I had, because I did pray about it "a little." But then my own desire to figure things out brought me to another conclusion. And I say all this to emphasize that I am not writing this on my own. It is the antithesis of any subject I've ever considered writing about. But like a jigsaw puzzle finally taking shape, I began to see how the themes of my dreams, especially over the last few years, have led to this assignment. I have repeatedly asked God what I should do with the piles of notebooks and journals containing my dreams. And just as His Word says, He answered.

"Call to me and I will answer you and tell you great and unsearchable things you do not know" (Jeremiah 33:3).

After the dream about the baby, I went back through my journals. Since embracing Christianity, the subjects of many of my dreams were disturbing: Prostitution. Adultery. Homosexuality. All Old Testament themes dealing with moral and spiritual apostasy—with turning away from God and His laws and instructions. Several dreams were about children and teeny, tiny babies. I now understand that many of those dreams were also messages. I have used some of them (unedited, just as I recorded them) to open the chapters in the rest of this book.

In addition, I have become increasingly burdened by the immoral direction our culture has taken. And I now believe that God has put this on my heart because it is on His. For the first time I truly understood the lyrics in the song, "Hosanna," that say, "Break my heart for what breaks Yours."[3] I now know that, while there is still time, God wants us to do the same thing He wanted and agreed to do for the people of Israel after hearing Solomon's prayer for them. God told Solomon that if they would "humble themselves and pray and seek my face and turn from their wicked ways, then will I hear from heaven and will forgive their sin and will heal their land" (2 Chronicles 7:14). The operative word in that verse is "if."

Solomon's prayer for the people of Israel—that they would repent and turn their hearts back to God—is this book's prayer for the United States of America. It is a prayer not about abortion per se, but about the underlying state of the human heart that says, "I can do anything I want. Anything I want to do is okay." It is a prayer for conviction of right choices.

I had never specifically brought my own abortions before the Lord because I had grouped them with all the other immoral things I'd done—and there were plenty. But after this revelation, God started to teach me, to show me, that what had been in my womb were babies, not inanimate objects that the words "embryos" or "fetuses" bring to mind. I kept thinking about that first part of Jeremiah 1:5, the Scripture verse in my dream: "I knew you before I formed you in your mother's womb..." That says that God is the author of life, that He designed the incredible process within our bodies that creates life. That means that He forms us, formed me, formed my babies, including the beautiful inside-and-out child that He allowed me to have.

When I applied that perspective to the awesome woman my daughter has become and thought about the other lives that were also in my womb, I ran to the bathroom. Crouched over the toilet, I was sickened by the realization that they would have been awesome, too. But I snuffed them out because they were inconveniences at the time. A time when I was having sex when I had no business having sex, and abortion was a way of not dealing with the consequences of what I was doing. Moreover, I was led to believe that what was inside of me wasn't really "living." But as this new revelation took hold, as I realized that I was just as pregnant with those babies as I had been with my daughter, each retch of my stomach became a wail of repentance.

I remembered how wonderful my full-term pregnancy was, and that I've never felt as good and as healthy as I did then. I've never felt as joyful, as happy, as wondrous at feeling a life moving and breathing inside of me. My sister reminds me of how much I laughed those nine months. And how I was so careful about what I ate and drank; that I wouldn't even chew gum because it had unnatural ingredients in it. The amazing thing to me now is that, as joyful as I was about that pregnancy, I don't remember thinking about the others at that time. I had become so indoctrinated by the culture, by feeling like there was nothing wrong with what I had done, that it didn't even matter.

I know now that, "I was shown mercy because I acted in ignorance and unbelief" (1 Timothy 1:13). Today I am so thankful to God for Jesus Christ, for His forgiveness, for the sacrifice of His perfect life for my oh-so-imperfect one. And because of that great exchange, "... as far as the east is from the west, so far has He removed our transgressions from us" (Psalm 103:12 NKJV). The lyrics of the song, "Amazing Love/You Are My King" say it best: "I'm forgiven because You were forsaken. I'm accepted, You were condemned. I'm alive and well, Your spirit lives within me because You died and rose again. Amazing love, how can it be, that You, my King, would die for me?"[4] It took time for me to understand this (although I will never fully comprehend it), and even more time to believe it.

It is said that grace is getting what we don't deserve and mercy is not getting what we do deserve. It was just this grace and mercy over my life, my brother's life, and the lives of people I love that led me to understand how much I need God. And I pray it is what will lead readers of this book to understand as well.

I realize that many will not believe me or the message I have been given, and that people will mock me and think me arrogant to say that I have heard from God. But the truth is that God is speaking to all of us, we are just not listening. In a devotional from *Our Daily Bread*, David McCasland says it best. "Are we listening for God's voice in our lives today? Are we more drawn by the vibration of a smartphone than the still, small voice of the Lord through His Word and His Spirit?"[5]

Anyone who knows me knows that I am a coward when it comes to public speaking. They also know that my history is one of an obsessive desire to please. Writing this book on this subject will assuredly expose me to criticism and derision. That is what I meant when I said that this book and its message is "my cross" to bear. But I am mortally afraid not to do what I am being directed to. Because as I was struggling with the enormity of what this message involves, and how unlike my nature and personality it is to be standing up and saying these things, I came across this Scripture:

"Whenever you hear me say something, warn them for me. If I say to the wicked, 'You are going to die,' and you don't sound the alarm warning them that it's a matter of life or death, they will die and it will be your fault. I'll hold you responsible. But if you warn the wicked and they keep right on sinning anyway, they'll most certainly die for their sin, but you won't die. You'll have saved your life" (Ezekiel 3:17-19 MSG).

And what is the warning? It is a final chance to choose between turning back to God and receiving His grace and mercy, or to continue turning our backs to Him and suffering the consequences.

Ever since I was a teenager I have had a strong desire to write. My professional career was anchored in writing. I've written and published some poetry, a few short stories, and helped a friend with her memoir. As I said earlier, I had started my own memoir when I was redirected by that dream. I know now that God is using the desire to write that He placed inside of me for His purpose.

In the September 30 devotional from *My Utmost for His Highest*, "The Assigning of the Call," Oswald Chambers says:

"We take our own spiritual consecration and try to make it into a call of God, but when we get right with Him He brushes all this aside. Then He gives us a tremendous, riveting pain to fasten our attention on something that we never even dreamed could be his call for us. And for one radiant, flashing moment we see His purpose, and we say, "Here am I! Send me" (Isaiah 6:8). [6]

Part Two

About Us

"So, go now and write all this down.
Put it in a book
So that the record will be there
to instruct the coming generations,
Because this is a rebel generation,
a people who lie,
A people unwilling to listen
to anything God tells them."
—Isaiah 30:8-9 (The Message)

June 1, 2011

I had a premature baby. It was a boy. Not sure how it happened, like it just came out, or maybe I was having an exam and they found/pulled it out. The baby was in a glass tube, like a vial. There was a controversy over feeding the baby, like a legal issue. I wasn't supposed to feed him because he was so small. Some said to just leave him alone to die naturally, that he was so premature anyway. But I felt like we should feed him, that maybe he would live, have a chance. But it wasn't clear how to do it because he was in the tube, and I didn't know how to get the food in, or what type of food to feed him. He was so tiny. I went up close to the tube and couldn't see his face clearly. It was like an ultrasound picture. But I started talking to him and he responded. Then I called a doctor. He was very happy to hear from me. He told me how to feed the baby. I was afraid because the baby was so small. But I was determined to try, to see if he would grow.

Chapter Six
Saving Trees, Killing Children

United States of America / Looks like another silent night/ As we're sung to sleep by philosophies / That save the trees and kill the children —from Casting Crowns song, "While You Were Sleeping." [7]

Come on, you say. What kind of a chapter title is that? Pretty extreme, isn't it? Who really wants to save trees but kill children?

Well, consciously, none of us do. Consciously, we know that a child, a human life, is inherently more valuable, more important, than a tree. But we have allowed semantics to override our innate, God-given sense of right and wrong. Paul Greenberg, Pulitzer Prize-winning editorial director of the *Arkansas Democrat Gazette*, puts it well in this quote from "Challenging the Language of the Culture of Death:"

> Those whom we want out of the way must first be dehumanized.... The least of these must be aborted in words before it becomes permissible to abort them in deed. [8]

The Roe vs. Wade ruling determined that a fetus is not a "person" as defined in the Fourteenth Amendment. [9] That's why I didn't feel as bad about aborting my babies back in the 1970s as I do now. As Mr. Greenberg explained, because we've "aborted" the concept of pre-born life, we have been desensitized into accepting the following procedure, performed in 80% of all abortions, during the first trimester, when babies have beating hearts,[10] can feel pain,[11] and become fully formed:[12]

> The abortionist first paralyzes the cervix and makes the womb opening. Then, he inserts a hollow plastic tube with a knife-like tip into the uterus. The tube is connected to a powerful pump with a suction force which is 29 times more powerful than a home vacuum cleaner. By Suction method, it actually tears the baby's body into pieces and the hose frequently pulls as pieces of the baby become lodged. The placenta is then cut from the inner wall of the uterus and scraps are sucked out into a bottle.[13]

Hard to read, isn't it? That's because this procedure is veiled beneath a sanitized term like "reproductive rights," and we've been mind-numbed into believing that a fetus is not a baby. Yet when we see an animal hit by a car or a baby bird that fell from its nest, our hearts are pierced with compassion.

In *American Grown: The Story of the White House Kitchen Garden and Gardens Across America,* Michelle Obama writes, "Just as each seed we plant has the potential to become something extraordinary, so does every child."[14] But apparently not the child in the womb.

A Matter of Convenience

"Do nothing out of selfish ambition or vain conceit, but in humility consider others better than yourselves" (Philippians 2:3).

The abortions I had weren't because there was a risk to my life or my babies' lives. It was because it was inconvenient for me to be pregnant. It was because I was too young and I was having unprotected, premarital sex. It was because I was led to think of the baby as a "nonperson." And "inconvenience" is the reason for the majority of abortions today. With statistics to support it, a 2011 report from the Guttmacher Institute says (emphasis mine):

> ...In any case, it is clear that the hard cases—rape, incest, life/health of mother or baby—are a very small fraction of cases. They are arguably a poor premise for formulating general public policy regarding abortion. At the other extreme, AGI's surveys of 1987 and 2004 (as well as the detailed statistics from Minnesota) suggest that **a significant fraction of abortions are obtained by mothers who have the means to care for a child but do not want their lives inconvenienced.** Even sex selective abortions may be more common than those for some of the hard cases. This illustrates the consequences of the current extreme policy in the United States regarding abortion. [15]

This is the reality. It's not about "reproductive rights" or "women's rights," it's about convenience and inconvenience. It's about sacrificing a child's life (because we're led to believe it isn't one) for our own.

On August 10, 2011, The *New York Times* published an article entitled, "The Two-Minus-One Pregnancy," about aborting one baby when twins are not wanted. This procedure (once again using sanitized terms) is called "pregnancy reduction" or "reduction to a singleton." The article opens with this paragraph:

> As Jenny lay on the obstetrician's examination table, she was grateful that the ultrasound tech had turned off the overhead screen. She didn't want to see the two shadows floating inside her. Since making her decision, she had tried hard not to think about them, though she could often think of little else. She was 45 and pregnant after six years of fertility bills, ovulation injections, donor eggs and disappointment — and yet here she was, 14 weeks into her pregnancy, choosing to extinguish one of two healthy fetuses, almost as if having half an abortion. As the doctor inserted the needle into Jenny's abdomen, aiming at one of the fetuses, Jenny tried not to flinch, caught between intense relief and intense guilt. [16]

Another part of the article continues:

> Even some people who support abortion rights admit to feeling queasy about reduction to a singleton. "I completely

respect and support a woman's choice," one commentator wrote on UrbanBaby. com, referring to a woman who said she reduced her pregnancy to protect her marriage and finances. One fetus was male, the other female, and the woman eliminated the male because she already had a son. "Something about that whole situation just seemed unethical to me," the commentator continued. "I just couldn't sleep at night knowing that I terminated my daughter's perfectly healthy twin brother." [17]

Why did Jenny feel guilt and why couldn't that woman sleep at night? The Apostle Paul says it's because they were created with an innate sense of right and wrong:

*"When outsiders who have never heard of God's law follow it more or less by instinct, they confirm its truth by their obedience. **They show that God's law is not something alien, imposed on us from without, but woven into the very fabric of our creation. There is something deep within them that echoes God's yes and no, right and wrong...**"* (Romans 2:14-15 MSG, emphasis mine).

Just because something is legal, doesn't mean it's moral. That's why I felt so horrible after my own abortion.

The historic Roe vs. Wade case was won based on a woman's "right to privacy" under the 14th Amendment, stating that it is a woman's decision, along with her doctor, whether or not to terminate her pregnancy.[18] And on the surface, this sounds fine. After all, what right does anyone have to tell a woman what she can and cannot do to with her own body? I would agree that is a private decision. A friend of mine once said, "You can't legislate morality." And that is correct. But what is needed in this country and around the world today is the same thing that was needed over two thousand years ago as the Apostle Paul preached to the Romans. We need to "not conform" any longer "to the pattern of this world, but be transformed by the renewing of [our] minds" (Romans 12:2 NIV). The Message version of the Bible puts it another way:

"Don't become so well-adjusted to your culture that you fit into it without even thinking. Instead, fix your attention on God. You'll be changed from the inside out. Readily recognize what he wants from you, and quickly respond to it. Unlike the culture around you, always dragging you down to its level of immaturity, God brings the best out of you, develops well-formed maturity in you" (Romans 12:2 MSG).

But because we have turned away from God, and what He tells us through His Word, the Bible, the problem is that we consider the life of the mother without considering the life of the child inside her. Byron White, the senior dissenting Judge in Roe vs. Wade, asserted that the Court:

> values the convenience of the pregnant mother more than the continued existence and development of the life or potential life that she carries.... I find nothing in the language or history of the Constitution to support the Court's judgment. The Court simply fashions and announces a new constitutional right for pregnant women and, with

scarcely any reason or authority for its action, invests that right with sufficient substance to override most existing state abortion statutes. The upshot is that the people and the legislatures of the 50 States are constitutionally disentitled to weigh the relative importance of the continued existence and development of the fetus, on the one hand, against a spectrum of possible impacts on the woman, on the other hand.[19]

And Andrew Napolitano, a former judge of the Superior Court of New Jersey says:

Did you catch that? The Supreme Court declared that the baby in the womb is not a person. When it made that declaration, it rejected dozens of decisions of other courts, in America and in Great Britain, holding that the baby in the womb is a person. This is reminiscent of the Supreme Court's infamous Dred Scott decision in 1857 in which it ruled that blacks were not persons. In both cases, it cited no precedent, it gave no rational basis, and in Roe vs. Wade, it merely said that because philosophers, physicians and lawyers could not agree on whether babies in wombs are persons, it would declare them not to be persons.... How scary is this? The Supreme Court declares a class of humanity not to be persons, and then permits people to destroy the members of the class. That's what happened to blacks during slavery; that was the philosophical argument underlying the Holocaust; that's what is happening to babies in the womb today; and that might become the basis for the government killing persons it hates or fears in the future. It will declare them to be non-persons.[20]

A Blinding Light

"...suddenly a light from heaven flashed around him"
(Acts 9:3).

If you know the Bible, you're familiar with the miraculous transformation of the Apostle Paul. He was known as Saul, a religious Jewish teacher who was zealous to snuff out the rise of Christianity. He persecuted and killed followers of Christ. He was on his way to Damascus to do just that when a blinding light threw him to the ground, and he had an encounter with Jesus.

Saul was blinded for three days, until a man named Ananias was directed by Jesus to lay hands on and pray for Saul. When Ananias prayed for him, something like scales fell from Saul's eyes, and he knew he had to preach the very Gospel he had been persecuting others for. Although Saul was Jewish, he was also a Roman citizen. "Saul" was his Hebrew name and "Paul" was his Gentile name, which he began using after this experience.[21] Paul, the most famous persecutor of Christians, wound up writing the majority of the New Testament.

A Modern-Day Apostle Paul

"Immediately, something like scales fell from Saul's eyes, and he could see again" (Acts 9:18).

Dr. Bernard Nathanson's story of transformation is second only to the Apostle Paul's. Dr. Nathanson, once known as "the father" of abortions, became this nation's staunchest pro-life advocate.

In 1969 Nathanson, a medical doctor certified in obstetrics and gynecology, co-founded the National Association for the Repeal of Abortion Laws (now known as the National Abortion Rights Action League, or NARAL). He was president of NARAL, and ran the largest abortion clinic in the United States, located on the upper east side of Manhattan. In an act of irony that only God could orchestrate, Dr. Nathanson could very well have performed my own abortions, as his clinic was most likely the one I would have gone to in the mid-1970s. If so, writing this book would be a direct manifestation of Romans 8:28, where God tells us that when we love Him, he works all things in our lives for good. *The Message* version of the Bible says, "He...knows our pregnant condition, and keeps us present before God. That's why we can be so sure that every detail in our lives of love for God is worked into something good." Though pregnancy is used symbolically in that translation, its applicability here is nonetheless startling.

In his book, *The Hand of God*, Dr. Nathanson describes the journey from aborting his own child to seeking the forgiveness found only through Jesus Christ for aborting a total of 75,000 children. From the late 1970s until his death in 2011, Dr. Nathanson became a champion for the unborn. The following is an excerpt from the part of the book where he describes his blinding light experience, and what made the scales fall from his eyes.

> I am personally responsible for 75,000 abortions. This legitimizes my credentials to speak to you with some authority on the issue. ... How did I change from prominent abortionist to pro-life advocate? I became director of obstetrics of a large hospital in New York City and had to set up a prenatal research unit, just at the start of a great new technology which we now use every day to study the fetus in the womb. A favorite pro-abortion tactic is to insist that the definition of when life begins is impossible; that the question is a theological or moral or philosophical one, anything but a scientific one. Fetology makes it undeniably evident that life begins at conception and requires all the protection and safeguards that any of us enjoy.... As a scientist I know, not believe, know that human life begins at conception. Although I am not a formal religionist, I believe with all my heart that there is a divinity of existence which commands us to declare a final and irreversible halt to this infinitely sad and shameful crime against humanity. [22]

Simple Arithmetic

"For the love of money is a root of all kinds of evil" (1 Timothy 6:10).

Many people have misinterpreted this verse. The Bible does not say that money, in itself, is evil. It says the "love of" money is at the root of evil. And once the scales were removed from Dr. Nathanson's eyes, he came to understand that about abortion.

> Why, you may well ask, do some American doctors who are privy to the findings of fetology, discredit themselves by carrying out abortions? Simple arithmetic at $300 a time. 1.55 million abortions means an industry generating $500,000,000 annually, of which most goes into the pocket of the physician doing the abortion. [23]

Pretty nauseating, isn't it? But the "simple arithmetic" Dr. Nathanson refers to is supported in a Feburary 4, 2012 *New York Times* article. In "The Media's Abortion Blinders," Ross Douthat says:

> Planned Parenthood likes to claim that abortion accounts for just 3 percent of its services, for instance, and this statistic has been endlessly recycled in the press. But the percentage of the group's clients who received an abortion is probably closer to 1 in 10, and Planned Parenthood's critics have estimated, plausibly, that between 30 and 40 percent of its health center revenue is from abortion. [24]

Hippocratic Hypocrites

"For the time will come when men will not put up with sound doctrine. Instead, to suit their own desires, they will gather around them a great number of teachers to say what their itching ears want to hear" (2 Timothy 4:3).

Also in his book, Dr. Nathanson reveals something that I'm sure many are unaware of. The original Hippocratic

Oath, the pledge all doctors take upon becoming a doctor, included the following:

> I will give no deadly medicine to anyone if asked, nor suggest any such counsel; and in like manner, I will not give to a woman a pessary (a device inserted in the vagina, thought erroneously to initiate an abortion) to produce an abortion. [25]

That original oath was written some 2500 years ago. Today it says this:

> Most especially must I tread with care in matters of life and death. If it is given to me to save a life, all thanks. But it may also be within my power to take a life; this awesome responsibility must be faced with great humbleness and awareness of my own frailty. Above all, I must not play at God. [26]

Again, how convenient. As Dr. Nathanson so aptly puts it:

> In a world as savage and primitive as was the Island of Cos in the year 450 B.C., the expression of compassion, of respect for one's teachers, for life itself was and remains a monument to the beauty of the human soul and the dignity of the human person. Such monuments should not be hastily abandoned. [27]

But we have abandoned that monument to life, haven't we? And that is crux of the message of this book. Because with the acceptance of abortion on demand, we have devalued life and what God says about it. And if life has no meaning, what else can possibly matter?

Our Moral Debt Ceiling

"On your clothes men find the lifeblood of the innocent poor.... Yet in spite of all this you say, 'I am innocent'.... But I will pass judgment on you because you say, 'I have not sinned'" (Jeremiah 2:34-35).

It seems that practically every year there is a political debate about the raising of America's debt ceiling. But what about our moral debt ceiling? The fact that over 57 million abortions have been performed since 1973, since the Roe vs. Wade ruling became law, indicates that we have reached it.[28] In 2013, when the number of abortions was 55 million, Carol Tobias, in an article called, "Endless Love" says:

> Fifty-five million children have been killed by abortion. It's difficult to comprehend that number. Almost 18% of our entire population, that number is equal to the population of the entire middle portion of the country. It's almost the population of New York and California.[29]

Who knows what those individuals—an average of 1.3 million a year—could have done for this country or the world? Maybe one held the solution to the economic and social problems we're having today. Maybe one could have thwarted 9/11. Maybe one could have found the cure for cancer. Think of it —the computer I'm writing on, the iPhones, iPads, iPods used and depended on all over the world, may not have been developed if Steve Jobs' birth mother decided to have an abortion, rather than give him up for adoption. And two of those innovators, two of those world-changers could very well have been my children. Or yours, if you are the mother or father of an aborted baby.

Had I known forty years ago what I know today, I either wouldn't have gotten pregnant, nor would I have had abortions. I would have lived according to God's Word and would have chosen life, as I hope and pray my own daughter and granddaughters will. That is why I am certain that the Lord is having me write this book at this time. Because the wave of immorality sweeping this nation, if left unheeded, will result in a tsunami of judgment.

Turn on your computer, iPhone, iPad, or flatscreen TV, and I dare you to watch for five minutes and not have something salacious assault your senses. Cybersex is a click away. This acceptance of and moral numbness toward sexual promiscuity has desensitized us further to its consequences.

As was stated earlier, statistics show that most abortions are performed not because of rape, incest, or harm to the mother or baby, but for birth control purposes. Like mine were. Does this seem right? Even to those who call themselves "pro choice"? To use abortion as birth control?

"Pro choice" proponents argue that the law cannot be allowed to regulate the choice a woman makes about her body. But what about the baby's body? I would argue that God is the original pro-choice proponent. He says in Deuteronomy 30:19, "I put before you life and death, choose life." We have a choice. The problem is, we have chosen to turn our backs on God and His Word and His teachings, and therefore our choices have become depraved, no different than two thousand years ago:

"...since they did not think it worthwhile to retain the knowledge of God, he gave them over to a depraved mind, to do what ought not to be done" (Romans 1:28).

Proverbs 16:25 says, "There is a way that seems right to a man, but in the end it leads to death." I thought my lifestyle was fine, even though it led to the killing of my children. Just as abortion on demand seems right to many, but in the end has led to the death of a generation.

 Dream Journal Entry
March 2, 2011

I was inside a building, looking out the window of a closed door. Three huge black bears were sleeping on the grass. I knew there were many children in the building, and was worried about what would happen when the bears woke up. There was a woman in charge, and I asked about the bears. The woman wasn't concerned, said they were harmless. But all I could think about were the children, and I woke up with a vision of the bears charging through the door and trampling them.

Chapter Seven
Slaughtering Innocents

"...they have filled this place with the blood of the innocent"
(Jeremiah 19:4).

On December 14, 2012, a troubled young man broke into Sandy Hook Elementary School in Newtown, Connecticut and mercilessly shot and killed twenty children, ages six and seven, and six adults. Although shootings have tragically become almost commonplace in America, this one caught the breath of the nation. The majority of its victims were children, many early reports referring to them as "babies."

Along with you, I was sickened by and incredulous at what happened at that school. I cried and my heart ached, still aches, for the families. Like others, I identified on a personal level—my granddaughter was the same age as the children who were killed. Because so many of my dreams have come to pass, I kept thanking God that I hadn't had a dream associated with that event. But horrifyingly, the next morning the dream on the facing page came to mind.

My heart beating wildly, I went through my journals and found the dream. When I checked the date, the world once again fell away. It was the night before the dream that birthed this book—about the baby in the bottle thrown in the trash. And I knew that the two were connected.

While talks of gun control, mental health reform, and curbing violence in the media dominated the national conversation, I came to understand that the answer God wants us to arrive at is one we have become blinded to. Rightfully, the thought of those innocent, defenseless children being mowed down in an environment assumed to be loving, nurturing, and protective was more than our collective consciousness could handle. But where were those children six and seven years before that horrible day? They were in an even more loving, nurturing, protective environment—they were in their mothers' wombs.

What is so different about what I did and what that young man did? What is so different about ripping a breathing, swallowing, heart-beating baby from its mother's womb and shooting a child who has been outside of the womb for six years? Some would say there is a huge difference, that there is no comparison. That the baby in the womb is subject to sacrifice at the altar of our convenience. But listen to what Tertullian, one of the leaders of the early church said:

> ...to kill a child before it is born is to commit murder by way of advance; and there is no difference whether you destroy a child in its formation, or after it is formed and delivered. For we Christians look upon him as a man, who is one in embryo; for he is in being, like the fruit in blossom, and in a little time would have been a perfect man, had nature met with no disturbance. [30]

And two thousand years later, Bernard Nathanson echoes this in his book, *The Hand of God*:

> Life is an interdependent phenomenon for all of us. It is a continuous spectrum which begins in utero and ends in death—the bands of the spectrum are designated by words such as fetus, infant, child, adolescent and adult. We must courageously face the fact—finally—that human life of a special order is being taken [in the process of abortion], and since the vast majority of pregnancies are carried successfully to term, abortion must be seen as the interruption of a process which would otherwise have produced a citizen of the world. Denial of this reality is the crassest kind of moral evasiveness. [31]

In his second inaugural speech in 2013, President Obama quoted from the Declaration of Independence:

> "We hold these truths to be self-evident, that all men are created equal, that they are endowed by their Creator with certain unalienable rights, that among these are Life, Liberty, and the pursuit of Happiness." [32]

With this statement, Mr. Obama affirmed what God says in the Bible:

"For you created my inmost being; you knit me together in my mother's womb.... My frame was not hidden from you when I was made in the secret place. When I was woven together in the depths of the earth, your eyes saw my unformed body. All the days ordained for me

69

were written in your book before one of them came to be"
(Psalm 139:13, 15-16).

Mr. Obama also said in his speech:

> "...Together, we resolved that a great
> nation must care for the vulnerable, and
> protect its people from life's worst hazards
> and misfortune..." [33]

I know the President was not thinking about the baby
in the womb when he said this, but is there anyone more
vulnerable?

Where Was God?

*"God is evicted from our culture and then He is blamed for
our carnages." —*Ravi Zacharias

News reports were saying that evil had visited
Newtown. Some even said the devil. But doesn't an
awareness of evil require an awareness of its opposite—
good? And doesn't an awareness of the devil require an
awareness of his opposite—God? So if we want and desire
good to prevail, which of course we do, then doesn't it stand
to reason that we should do what God says? But we're not.
Yet after Newtown many were asking, "Where was God?"
or "How could God have let this happen?"

Here's what I've learned:

God is the author and Creator of life. The devil is the
author and cause of death. Jesus says, "The thief comes

only to steal and kill and destroy; I have come that they may have life, and have it to the full" (John 10:10). Like the Apostle Paul and Bernard Nathanson, we need to have the scales removed from our eyes. **Because we are recognizing the one who takes life, but not the One who gives it**.

There is a legend about a Cherokee elder who was teaching his grandchildren about life. He said to them, "A fight is going on inside me... It is a terrible fight between two wolves. One wolf represents fear, anger, envy, sorrow, regret, greed, arrogance, hatefulness, and lies. The other stands for joy, peace, love, hope, humbleness, kindness, friendship, generosity, faith, and truth. This same fight is going on inside of you, and inside every other person, too." The children thought about it for a minute. Then one child asked his grandfather, "Which wolf will win?" The Cherokee elder replied... "The one you feed."

The day after the massacre, Tom Ascol, Executive Director of Founders Ministries, put it this way:

> The roots of Sandy Hook and Aurora and Columbine and all of the other senseless violence in our nation are not primarily related to the availability of guns. They are primarily related to the evil that lurks in every human heart because of moral and spiritual brokenness. What needs to be meaningfully considered and deeply studied is the way that official actions of our nation over the last fifty years have nurtured and cultivated those roots so that they are now blossoming

more and more in the murderous actions of people—especially young people—like Adam Lanza. [34]

The spiritual brokenness he refers to is the same human condition that the Apostle Paul addresses in his letter to the Romans:

"They exchanged the truth of God for a lie, and worshiped and served created things rather than the Creator ... They have become filled with every kind of wickedness, evil, greed and depravity. They are full of envy, murder, strife, deceit and malice" (Romans 1:25, 29).

And Ravi Zacharias, one of the world's best-known and respected Christian Apologists, penned this just days after Newtown in his article, "Tragedy at Newtown" (emphasis mine):

As for the entertainment world, what does one even say at a time like this? Calling for gun control and then entertaining the masses with bloodshed is only shifting the focus from law to entertainment. Do our entertainers ever pause to ask what debased values emerge from their stories? The death of decency is audible and visible in what passes as movie entertainment and political speech. This is the same culture that wishes to take away Nativity scenes and Christmas carols from our children. **God is evicted from our culture and then He is blamed for our carnages. America is lost on the high seas of time, without chart or compass. The storms that await us will sink**

**this nation beyond recognition if we
do not awaken to the rapid repudiation of the values that shaped this
nation. The handwriting is on the
wall. Freedom is not just destroyed
by its retraction. It is destroyed even
more painfully by its abuse.** [35]

And what could be a more blatant abuse of our
freedom of choice than to, instead of choosing life as God
instructs, turn it into a sacrificial sacrament for our own
convenience.

Child Sacrifice: Are We Any Better?

*"Shall I offer my firstborn for my transgression, the fruit of
my body for the sin of my soul?"* (Micah 6:7).

We think of ourselves as so much more sophisticated
and advanced than people in Biblical times. But let's take
a look at the city of Carthage during the time of the prophet
Isaiah, as described by Matt Black in a sermon from Living
Hope Bible Church.

It is a city on the tip of northern Africa,
just east of modern day Algeria. It was the
capital of the Carthaginian Empire, one of
the longest-living and largest empires in
the ancient Mediterranean...At the height
of the empire, Carthage was the most
sophisticated, well-educated, militarily
superior, and technologically advanced
nation in the ancient world. And yet in
all their sophistication, knowledge, and

advancement, they were also destroying millions of babies in child sacrifice each year. [36]

In that sermon, Mr. Black references a modern historian, P. G. Mosca, who asks of the ancient people of Carthage:

> ...how could a culture so well developed morally, intellectually and materially tolerate so 'abominable' a custom? How could a sophisticated people sanction what seems to be such a barbaric practice for so long a time? How at the most [intimate] and critical level could human parents bring about the destruction of their own child? [37]

The practice of child sacrifice, though prohibited by Mosaic law, is documented throughout the Old Testament. And it was detestable to God:

"...they have filled this place with the blood of the innocent. They have built the high places of Baal to burn their sons in the fire as offerings to Baal—something I did not command or mention, nor did it enter my mind..." (Jeremiah 19:4-5 NIV).

But it entered their minds then and it enters our minds today. Surprisingly, in much the same way.

As I was watching Bill O'Reilly's program one night, he referred to a column he had written entitled, "What the Babies Would Say." It was in response to another column that posited that even if a fetus is a human life, the woman carrying that fetus is "the boss." And her rights, circumstances and decisions should outweigh any rights of the child inside her.

Part of Mr. O'Reilly's response was:

> We are not talking about life endan-germent or catastrophic damage to the mother here. No. What [the author] believes, and she's not alone, is that a woman can execute her fetus simply because "she's the boss." [38]

But the Bible says we are not the boss. "You are not your own; you were bought at a price. Therefore honor God with your body" (1 Corinthians 6:19-20). But not only have we dishonored God with our bodies by offering "the fruit of our body for the sin of our soul" (Micah 6:7) just as the people of Carthage did, we have completely abandoned God. We have become so accustomed to doing and having things our own way that we rarely consider alternatives that might inconvenience us or inhibit our self-gratification. Just as I didn't change my lifestyle after my first abortion, many women today are of the same mindset.

What is wrong with us? Why do we ignore everything God tells us about how to live in a just and moral way? Maybe it's because so many of us are like I was—ignorant of what it is that God is saying.

 Dream Journal Entry

January 3, 2012

On line in a grocery/delicatessen. People ordering corned beef and cabbage. Wondered if it was St. Patrick's Day. Behind the counter, next to where they were serving the corned beef and cabbage, there was a big piece of raw meat shaped like a cow. The part of its head where its mouth would be was opening and closing, like it was trying to talk. Looked really weird. I got out of the line and went to a room where the manager was to alert him about the raw meat. I thought he'd want to know about it and that no one was asking for it. The manager said he did know, but everyone wanted the corned beef instead.

Chapter Eight
Ignoring Knowledge

"...my people are destroyed from lack of knowledge" (Hosea 4:6).

How like our culture is that delicatessen?

God's Word, the Bible, in all of its "raw meat," is available and speaking to us. But we either ignore it completely or "cook" it to our liking, boil it like corned beef, until it gives us what our "itching ears want to hear" (2 Timothy 4:3). Some call this "cafeteria Christianity," picking and choosing what we like from the Bible, and ignoring the rest. This ignorance of God's Word, this turning our backs on God, is what He says will destroy us. And in the Bible it is compared to betrayal, much like adultery.

Committing Adultery

"'Return, faithless people,' declares the LORD, 'for I am your husband'" (Jeremiah 3:14).

Throughout the Old Testament, God's relationship with Israel is described as a love relationship, a marriage. Almighty God as the husband and Israel, His people, the wife. This analogy is used time and again to show us how, just as a husband or wife can be unfaithful to their spouse, so we can be unfaithful to God.

One of the best examples is in the book of Hosea. God commanded the prophet to take "an adulterous wife" (1:2) to illustrate Israel's spiritual infidelity to God. Hosea's wife runs after other men, while Israel runs after other gods. His wife commits physical adultery, while Israel commits spiritual adultery. It is interesting that God chooses our strongest human desire—sex—to describe His relationship with us. Sexual imagery is used to show how strong our passions are for things in our lives that compete with our relationship with God. "Have you seen what faithless Israel has done? She has gone up on every high hill and under every spreading tree and has committed adultery there" (Jeremiah 3:6).

Who or what are we committing spiritual adultery with? I would venture to say that for most of us, it is with ourselves. We put our own needs and desires at the forefront of our lives, without considering what God wants, which is a loving relationship with us. And when we refuse that relationship, or put anything else above it, the Bible says God is jealous. "Do not worship any other god, for the LORD, whose name is Jealous, is a jealous God" (Exodus 34:14). "Do not follow other gods, the gods of the peoples around you; for the LORD your God, who is among you, is a jealous God and his anger will burn against you, and he will destroy you from the face of the land" (Deuteronomy 6:14-15).

Because I had no idea who the real God was, I "followed the gods of the peoples around me." In my case, I sought to fill the God-shaped hole in my heart through New Age gurus like Wayne Dyer, Anthony Robbins, and Marianne Williamson. But it wasn't until I discovered Jesus Christ and His words, "I am the way, the truth, and the life..." (John 14:6 NKJV) that the hole began to fill. And when that started to happen, God had compassion on me, the same way He did on those who repented in Hosea's day, "I will heal their waywardness and love them freely, for my anger has turned away from them" (14:4). But for those who did not and will not repent He says, "I will have no compassion..." (13:14).

And that's where the importance of the message of this book comes in. The message to repent and turn to God, because "it is a dreadful thing to fall into the hands of the living God" (Hebrews 10:31). The problem is, many of us don't know what God wants, because we don't read His Word, like I didn't.

Like many of us, Israel had broken their covenant with God, worshipped other gods, and had "exchanged their Glory (i.e., God) for something disgraceful" (Hosea 4:7). That's why God says through Hosea, "my people are destroyed from lack of knowledge" (Hosea 4:6). But what knowledge is God talking about? It is knowledge of Himself, His principles of life that come only through following the roadmap to life that He has left us, the Bible. Without that knowledge, Scripture says, we will perish: "...a people without understanding will come to ruin" (Hosea 4:14). But to know the God of the Bible in any way, and particularly to understand what God wants to show us, we need to first come to grips with a few basic principles.

Fire and Brimstone...or Truth?

"This is a hard teaching. Who can accept it?" (John 6:60).

I never sought understanding of Biblical principles because they seemed so Old-Testament-fire-and-brimstone that I felt they didn't apply to me. But "a lack of knowledge" of these principles is what kept me away for the first 53 years of my life. Therefore I believe it is foundational to first understand what they are. So before going any further, let's look at seven definitions from a Biblical point of view, with a layperson's understanding:

- Sin/Sinner
- Lust
- Flesh
- Pride
- Repentance
- Humility
- Redemption

Sin/Sinner

"For all have sinned and fall short of the glory of God" (Romans 3:23).

Until 2004, I didn't feel like a sinner. I felt like a "good" person—doing my best to be a faithful wife, mother, sister, aunt, and friend. Whenever I'd hear preachers talking about "sin" and "repentance," it seemed as if they were talking about murderers, adulterers, and rapists—not me. And the definition of "sin" in Merriam-Webster's Dictionary goes along with that thinking: "an offense against religious or moral law; an action that is or is felt to be highly reprehensible; an often serious shortcoming; a transgression of the law of God."

When we read this, we tend to think of Ten Commandments stuff like murder and robbery. And yes, those are sins. But when you take the word "sin" (and the others we are about to look at) as it was used in its original languages of Hebrew and Greek, we are presented with a whole new understanding, one that is essential to the Gospel message.

The word "sin" in Greek, the original language of the New Testament, is "hamartia." The word "hamartia" is rooted in the notion of "missing the mark," [39] like in archery.

> The Hebrew word for sin is "chet," which, also, literally means "**missing the mark**" (emphasis mine). According to Jewish beliefs, a person sins when he or she goes astray. A sin could be actively doing something wrong, such as stealing, or it could be not doing something, such as walking past a person in need when you could help them. [40]

So basically, the word "sin" means to choose to do something wrong, or not to do something right. It is what the Apostle Paul meant when he said in Romans 3:23, "for all have sinned and fall short of the glory of God." The new Living Translation puts it even better, clearer: "For everyone has sinned; we all fall short of God's glorious standard." In other words, it means that no one (except God) is perfect. Who reading this can say they've never told a lie, never had a bad thought, never cheated—even a tiny bit?

The word "sinner" is interchangeable with the word "human."

Flesh

"...the spirit indeed is willing, but the flesh is weak" (Matthew 26:41 KJV).

One of the definitions of this word from Merriam-Webster is "the physical nature of human beings." In Greek the word is "sarx": "the flesh, denotes mere human nature, the earthly nature of man apart from divine influence, and therefore prone to sin and opposed to God."[41] In Hebrew the word is "basar": "of the body; flesh as frail or erring (man against God)." [42]

As "sinner" is interchangeable with "human," "flesh" is interchangeable with "humanity."

Pride

"Pride goes before destruction, a haughty spirit before a fall" (Proverbs 16:18).

Merriam-Webster defines pride as "the quality or state of being proud; inordinate self-esteem: conceit." The main Hebrew root is ge-ah [גֵּאָה]; the most common term is ga-on [גָּאוֹן]. Included are the ideas of arrogance, cynical insensitivity to the needs of others, and presumption. Pride is both a disposition/attitude and a type of conduct.[43]

In Greek, the meaning is "empty, braggart talk; an insolent and empty assurance, which trusts in its own power and resources and shamefully despises and violates divine laws and human rights; an impious and empty presumption which trusts in the stability of earthy [*sic*] things."[44]

There is a good kind of pride that shouldn't be confused with what we're talking about here. It's okay and good to be proud of your children, or to take pride in a job well done—a healthy, balanced sort of pride. The Biblical pride we're getting at is being self-focused. It is interchangeable with "it's all about me." And pride is what is at the root of all sin. It is the foundational reason we "miss the mark." And it is the thing God hates above all, even more than the most detestable acts, because pride is what launches them. It is what gives birth to the attitude that we can do and justify anything we want. Proverbs 6:16-19 talks about the things the Lord hates, and the first one is "a proud look" (KJV).

Lust

"For everything in the world—the cravings of sinful man, the lust of his eyes and the boasting of what he has and does—comes not from the Father but from the world" (1 John 2:16).

Merriam-Webster defines lust as "pleasure, delight, personal inclination, intense sexual desire." Though those don't sound like necessarily bad things, it is, again, in the original Biblical languages that we find the applicable meaning.

The Hebrew/Aramaic origin: "avah": "desire, incline, covet, wait longingly, wish, sigh, want, be greedy, prefer; (Piel) to desire, crave (food and drink); (Hithpael) to desire, long for, lust after (of bodily appetites)."[45] The Greek origin: "epithymia": "desire, craving, longing, desire for what is forbidden." [46]

In the Old Testament, lust is usually referred to in terms of idolatry, when people yearned or lusted after other/false gods. At the same time, it also speaks of sexual immorality. "And yet they would not hearken unto their judges, but they went a whoring [prostituting/lusting] after other gods, and bowed themselves unto them: they turned quickly out of the way which their fathers walked in, obeying the commandments of the LORD; but they did not so" (Judges 2:17 KJV).

In the book of 1 John, we are reminded that the world and its desires (lusts) pass away, whereas "the man who does the will of God lives forever" (2:16-17). This is saying that our "lusts" are in direct violation of God's perfect will, because they usually are misdirected, moving and leading us away from God to our own selfish desires.

Humility

"Humble yourselves before the Lord and he will lift you up" (James 4:10).

Merriam-Webster defines humility as "not proud or haughty : not arrogant or assertive; reflecting, expressing, or offered in a spirit of deference or submission; ranking low in a hierarchy or scale : insignificant, unpretentious."

In Hebrew/Aramaic, humility is "anavah": "humility, gentleness, meekness." [47] In Greek, it is "tapeinophrosynē": "the state of having 'a humble opinion of one's self,' a 'deep sense of one's moral littleness,' or 'lowliness of mind.'"[48] In Matthew 11:29, Jesus says He is "meek and lowly." Humility is the opposite of pride.

Repentance

"And so John came...preaching a baptism of repentance for the forgiveness of sins" (Mark 1:4).

Wikipedia defines this best, including both the Greek and Hebrew definitions. This is a foundational principle, so I think it's worth a longer explanation.

Repentance is the activity of reviewing one's actions and feeling contrition or regret for past wrongs. It generally involves a commitment to personal change and resolving to live a more responsible and humane life. In religious contexts it usually refers to confession to God, ceasing sin against God in order to gain forgiveness or absolution. It typically includes an admission of guilt, a promise or resolve not to repeat the offense; an attempt to make restitution for the wrong, or in some way to reverse the harmful effects of the wrong where possible.

In Biblical Hebrew, the idea of repentance is represented by two verbs: שׁוּב shuv (to return) and נחם nicham (to feel sorrow). In the New Testament, the word translated as 'repentance' is the Greek word μετάνοια (metanoia), "after/behind one's mind", which is a compound word of the preposition 'meta' (after, with), and the verb 'noeo' (to perceive, to think, the result of perceiving or observing). In this compound word the preposition combines the two meanings of time and change, which may be denoted by 'after' and 'different'; so that the whole compound means: 'to think differently after'. Metanoia is therefore primarily an afterthought, different from the former thought; a change of mind accompanied by regret and change of conduct, "change of mind and heart", or, "change of consciousness." A description of repentance in the New Testament can be found in the parable of the prodigal son found in the Gospel of Luke (15 beginning at verse 11). [49]

Redemption

"In him we have redemption through his blood, the forgiveness of sins..." (Ephesians 1:7).

Wikipedia says, "Redemption is a religious concept referring to forgiveness or absolution for past sins or errors and protection from damnation and disgrace, eternal or temporary, generally through sacrifice." [50]

In Hebrew, the word is "pĕduwth" which means "ransom." [51] In Greek, the word is "apolytrōsis," which means "a releasing effected by payment of ransom; redemption, deliverance; liberation procured by the payment of a ransom." [52] Jesus paid the ransom of His life to redeem us from "damnation and disgrace" so that we can have a direct relationship with Our Father in Heaven. This unbelievable reality is summed up in John 3:16: "For God so loved the world [you and me] that He gave His only begotten Son [Jesus], that whoever believes in Him should not perish but have everlasting life" (NKJV).

In Summary:

Term	Meaning	Application
Sin	Missing the mark	What we do
Flesh	Human nature	Who/what we are
Pride	Conceit, Haughtiness	How we are/act
Lust	Desire, covet	What we do/want
Humility	Meekness, Gentleness	What we need to have
Repentance	Change of mind, heart	What we need to do
Redemption	Deliverance, Ransom	What Jesus did/does

My "lack of knowledge" of these principles directly contributed to the destruction of my children, and the lifestyle that led up to it. Now that we have demystified the salvation message, let's look at how those words of Hosea apply to our culture today: "My people are being destroyed because they don't know me" (Hosea 4:6a NLT).

August 4, 2012

I was walking outside. A woman came running to me, saying that there were children in the house across the street who were either in trouble/danger, or doing something they shouldn't be. Think she was afraid to do anything about it. I asked, "Did you tell anyone about it?" But she hadn't. So I went across the street to the house. It was a small, gray cedar shake house, Cape Cod-looking. It had a big banner across the front, under the roof, with the words: "AMERICAN HOUSE" in red letters. I opened the door. It was disgusting. Children/young adults. Sloppy, naked and dirty. Sitting around drinking. Some were obviously drunk. I didn't say anything, just looked. Then someone said, "She's seen us! Now we have to get her!" Like to make sure I wouldn't tell anyone. I knew they were going to come after me, maybe try to kill me. I got really scared and ran from the house and called 911.

Chapter Nine
Becoming Godless

"They have set up their detestable idols in the house that bears my Name and have defiled it" (Jeremiah 7:30).

"In God We Trust" has been the official motto of the United States of America since 1956.[53] But today God is saying, "These people honor me with their lips, but their hearts are far from me" (Matthew 15:8 quoting Isaiah 29:13). Isaiah and Jesus could have been addressing the 2012 Democratic Convention.

Aside from professing Catholics like Caroline Kennedy speaking in favor of abortion (a.k.a. "reproductive rights"), a controversy erupted at the convention after the news media reported that the word "God," which had been included in the previous year's platform, had been removed from 2012's. After much clamor and a vote that was clearly not decisive, the word was added back. The democratic platform, upon which the then current President (Obama) stood, attempted to say, "There is no God." The Bible tells us only fools say that: "The fool says in his heart, 'There is no God'" (Psalm 14:1).

So what happens when this statement starts to make its way into the national conversation? The same thing that Paul warned the Corinthians: "Don't you know that a little yeast works through the whole batch of dough?" (1 Corinthians 5:6).

In Chapter Seven, I quoted Tom Ascol referring to the "official actions of our nation" and Ravi Zacharias to the "repudiation of values" that have led to our downward moral spiral. A spiral that breeds disturbed young men who murder and has bottomed out at 57 million dead Americans. Besides abortion on demand, below are other "official actions" and "repudiation of values," more "yeast," if you will, and their unintended but inevitable consequences.

In 1962 the United States Supreme Court prohibited the saying of this simple non-denominational prayer in public schools: "Almighty God, we acknowledge our dependence upon Thee, and we beg Thy blessing upon us, our teachers, and our country."

In 1963 the Supreme Court banned Bible teaching in public schools.

In 1980 the Supreme Court ordered the public schools to remove the Ten Commandments from student view.

Since those laws were enacted, the following statistics show their effect:

SAT scores	down	**10%**
Teen suicide	up	**450%**
Child abuse	up	**2300%**
Illegal drugs	up	**6000%**
Criminal arrests of teens 14-17	up	**150%**
Divorce	up	**350%**
Birth to unmarried girls under 20	up	**150%**. [54]

The Bible says, "Do not be deceived: God cannot be mocked. A man reaps what he sows" (Galatians 6:7-8). Let's take a look at the morality of our nation today, and see how this truth has played itself out.

Friends With Benefits

"They exchanged the truth of God for a lie..." (Romans 1:25).

The 2011 film, "Friends with Benefits," was a huge hit with young people. The plot revolves around a young woman and man who meet in New York City and naively believe adding sex to their friendship will not lead to complications. Over time, they begin to develop deep mutual feelings for each other, only to deny it each time they are together.

In other words, adding sex did lead to "complications." In my case, it led to pregnancy and abortion. In the movie, the "complications" were emotional attachment and falling in love. Why? Because God created sex to be enjoyed within the context of —yes—emotional attachment and falling in love, but under the umbrella of marriage. Which is what was missing in this movie. And what is missing in millions of relationships today.

Having sex means becoming as physically close as you can possibly get to another human being. If you are a woman, the man is, literally, inside of you. If you are a man, you are, literally, inside of the woman. That is what God means when he says, "For this reason a man will leave his father and mother and be united to his wife, **and they will become one flesh**" (Genesis 2:24, emphasis mine). This is a clear establishment of the Biblical definition of marriage.

To believe it's okay to have sex in a casual way, like shaking hands, is a lie that has disguised itself as truth. It is a lie I believed as a young woman, a lie that millions believe today, a lie that keeps abortion clinics and pharmaceutical houses profitable. It is the lie that has brought us to our moral debt ceiling, invading our culture, deceiving our children and breeding headlines like the following, taken from the Good Morning America website.

<u>Oral Sex Is the New Goodnight Kiss</u>

"Are they ashamed of their loathsome conduct? No, they have no shame at all; they do not even know how to blush" (Jeremiah 8:12).

> In the documentary from Canadian filmmaker Sharlene Azam, "Oral Sex Is the New Goodnight Kiss," girls as young as 11 years old talk about having sex, going to sex parties and—in some extreme situations— crossing into prostitution by exchanging sexual favors for money, clothes or even homework and then still arriving home in time for dinner with the family. "Five minutes and I got $100," one girl said. "If I'm going to sleep with them, anyway, because they're good-looking, might as well get paid for it, right?" Another girl talked about being offered $20 to take off her shirt or $100 to do a striptease on a table at a party. "The

> prettiest girls from the most successful families [are the most at risk]. We're not talking about marginalized girls," Azam said. "[Parents] don't want to know because they really don't know what to do. I mean, you might be prepared to learn that, at age 12, your daughter has had sex, but what are you supposed to do when your daughter has traded her virginity for $1,000 or a new bag?[55]

As the mother of a daughter and the grandmother of three girls, this was hard for me to read. But this is where the "Friends with Benefits"—the "there is no God" mindset leads.

We Don't Want Boundaries

"'I have the right to do anything,' you say—but not everything is beneficial. 'I have the right to do anything'—but not everything is constructive" (1 Corinthians 10:23 TNIV).

People—maybe even you—dismiss or laugh off the concept of "original sin." But when we strive to become our own god, when we say, "She's the boss" about the pregnant woman, as abortion rights activists do,[56] we're doing exactly what the Bible says Adam and Eve did.

In the Garden of Eden, God "... made all kinds of trees grow out of the ground—trees that were pleasing to the eye and good for food. In the middle of the Garden were the tree of life and the tree of the knowledge of good and evil ... and the LORD GOD commanded the man, 'You are free to eat from any tree in the garden; but you must not eat from the tree of the knowledge of good and evil, for when you eat of it you will surely die'" (Genesis 2:9, 16-17).

God told Adam (who told Eve) that they were free to eat fruit from any tree in the garden, except for one, and what would happen if he/they disobeyed. But the serpent came along and questioned God's instruction, asking Eve, "Did God really say, 'You must not eat from any tree in the garden?'" (Genesis 3:1). Eve then corrected him, pointing out the direction about just the one tree, and that if she ate from it she would die. But the serpent told her that she wouldn't die, that God knew that if she ate it, she would be like God, knowing good and evil. So she examined the fruit, it looked like it would taste good and make her smart, so she ate it. And then gave some to Adam. "Then the eyes of both of them were opened and they realized they were naked; so they sewed fig leaves together and made coverings for themselves" (Genesis 3:7).

Before Adam and Eve ate the fruit, they thought nothing of being naked. It was perfectly natural for them. But after they did what God told them not to do, they felt shame, and tried to cover it up. That is what conscience is. Feeling bad or ashamed about doing something we're not supposed to do. It is what I felt after my abortion. It is innate and God-given. And it is what, as a nation, we need to reclaim.

God did not tell Adam and Eve they couldn't eat fruit from any of the trees—just one tree. He established a boundary. Similarly, God is not telling us we cannot have sex—He created sex. If you think God is a prude, listen to this, from Song of Songs, where Solomon is talking to his wife: "How beautiful you are and how pleasing, O love with your delights! Your stature is like that of the palm, and your breasts like clusters of fruit ... I will climb the palm tree; I will take hold if its fruit. May your breasts be like the clusters of the vine, the fragrance of your breath like apples, and your mouth like the best wine" (7:6-9).

God is saying we can have all the sex we want, only within the boundary of Biblical marriage: "This explains why a man leaves his father and mother and is joined to his wife, and the two are united into one." (Genesis 2:24 NLT). Because if we have sex outside of that boundary, as I did, we will get pregnant, have abortions, get STDs, and the list goes on and on. But the devil comes along and says, "Did God really say that you cannot have sex? Those things will surely not happen to you." But like Eve, we see that a man or a woman or a situation is "pleasing to the eye, and also desirable for gaining wisdom" (Genesis 3:6 TNIV) or for making us feel good, or for making money or gaining popularity. And we have reached the point where we continue to not only eat the forbidden fruit, but to glorify it.

Parading Our Sins

"...they parade their sin like Sodom; they do not hide it. Woe to them!" (Isaiah 3:9 TNIV).

Unfortunately, there are many modern-day examples of Isaiah's depiction of human depravity. Two that come to mind are Miley Cyrus' performance at the VMA awards in August 2013, and the 2013 Oscar-nominated movie, "Wolf of Wall Street."

From 2006 to 2011, Miley Cyrus, the then teen-aged daughter of country singer Billy Ray Cyrus, either won or was nominated for both the Teen Choice Awards and Nickelodeon Kids' Choice Awards for her role in the Disney television series, "Hannah Montana." According to Wikipedia, The Teen Choice Awards are voted on by viewers aged 13 to 19. The Nickelodeon Kids' Choice Awards are voted on by even younger viewers.

At the 2013 MTV Video Music Awards, Miley Cyrus (then 20 years old) pranced across the stage practically naked. Her hair was fixed into two knot-like horns atop her head and her tongue swirled in nonstop reptilian motion. Using an oversized foam hand and her performance partner, Robin Thicke, as props, this idol to thousands— if not millions—of little girls, simulated every imaginable sexual act.

We even have a word now to describe what she was doing: "twerking." Defined by Urbandictionary.com, it is "the rhythmic gyrating of the lower fleshy extremities in a lascivious manner with the intent to elicit sexual arousal or laughter in ones intended audience." How many thousands of those teen and preteen fans who voted for Miley's performance as Hannah Montana just a few years before do you think were watching that performance? And as if her exposition wasn't bad enough, Miley was singing her then new single, "We Can't Stop," a song celebrating a house party and recreational drug use. Here are some of the lyrics and descriptions of the song, found on Wikipedia:

> It's our party, we can do what we want/
> It's our party, we can say what we want/
> It's our party, we can love who we want/
> We can kiss who we want/ We can live how we want. [57]

Do we really want our children twerking to these lyrics in the shower?

> The song also makes several references to recreational drug use, including "dancing with molly", using a slang term for ecstasy, and "trying to get a line [of cocaine] in the bathroom". After initial confusion whether the former lyric was "dancing with molly" or "dancing with Miley," Cyrus clarified that she was referring to ecstasy, commenting that "if you're aged ten it's 'Miley', if you know what I'm talking about then you know. I just wanted it to be played on the radio and they've already had to edit it so much.[58]

The "Wolf of Wall Street" is another example of how the prophet Isaiah's exposition applies today. This Oscar-nominated movie depicts the life of Jordan Belfort, a self-made Wall Street swindler. Besides using the F-word over 500 times, below is a sampling of what is in this movie:

> Crude jokes involving bodily functions and various sexual acts are present throughout, and the number of graphic sex scenes in Wolf of Wall Street are well into the double digits. The majority of these sequences feature graphic nudity (including more fully nude women with breasts and lower regions exposed to count, male rear nudity, etc.) and very realistic portrayals of sex of all kinds—oral and anal relations included. Sex with prostitutes and with multiple partners at the same time is regularly shown in the film, and illegal drugs often make their way into sexual situations as well with Jordan sniffing cocaine off a prostitute's bare behind in one scene and another woman's breasts later on. A woman walks into an orgy of gay men who are all naked and engaging in various homosexual acts. A man is also shown masturbating at an office party (his erect penis is briefly shown). While Jordan is fully naked, he gives himself an enema with a candle.[59]

This review was from Crosswalk.com, an online Christian site. They titled their review, "Man's Depravity Knows No Bounds," and they inexorably bash this film:

> Taking self-indulgence to an entirely new level (and no, that's not a compliment), what remains is a soulless, revolting and wildly unfocused celebration of excess where nobody wins by watching...But more than anything, what's missing from The Wolf of Wall Street is a conscience, a crack of light in this dismal affair. If you're going to justify showing such deplorable behavior, you'd better have a compelling reason for it. Unfortunately, Scorsese seems content just stumbling in the dark.[60]

Yet *Christianity Today*, a purportedly Christian magazine, gave this film three and a half out of their top four-star rating. Their chief film critic, Alissa Wilkinson, says this, in part, about the film:

> Let's be clear: The Wolf of Wall Street is a great and possibly terrific movie, as movies go, one of the best Scorsese has made in a long while. It makes no sense for a three-hour movie in which you basically know what will happen to be this engrossing.... *Wolf* is also very funny.... [61]

Ms. Wilkinson does make some caveats in her review about graphic content. However, when a magazine with "Christianity" in its title uses adjectives like "terrific," "best," "engrossing" and "funny" to describe this movie, we have the epitome of an oxymoron. What better example of our schizophrenic attitude toward morality?

The "Wolf of Wall Street" was given an R rating, defined by the Motion Picture Association of America (MPAA) as:

"Restricted. Children Under 17 Require Accompanying Parent or Adult Guardian." Note the word "children." The MPAA is admitting that a 17-year-old is a child. And they are allowing those children unrestricted access to what should never come before their eyes. Additionally, children under 17 can see the movie if accompanied by an adult. It seems that this movie should have been given at least an NC-17 rating, which means "No One 17 and Under Admitted." Martin Scorsese actually had to cut some scenes to avoid this rating.

> There's still enough sex in "The Wolf of Wall Street" even though director Martin Scorsese had to trim some footage in order to avoid an NC-17 rating in the US, which would have substantially limited the audience for the film that portrays the sex-and-drugs excess of Wall Street in the late '80s. [62]

It seems Mr. Scorsese is more interested in profits than protecting children. I wonder if he realizes, or even cares, that his movies feed a culture that continues to believe it's okay to kill a baby in the womb, a culture that has become numb to news stories like these:

School Surveys 7th Graders on Oral Sex

> A middle school in Massachusetts is under fire for requiring children to complete a graphic sex survey—without parental knowledge or consent—that included questions about sexual partners and oral sex.[63]

Morning-After Pills Available to N.Y. High School Students

Hundreds of New York City high schools students have received morning-after pills since the launch of a program that provides emergency contraception through public school nurses, the city's health department said on Monday.

Many schools around the nation have long made condoms available to students but New York health officials said they believe the city is the first to make hormonal contraceptives available.

The program, which started last year and now has been instituted at 13 high schools, allows school nurses to give students emergency contraceptive pills, designed to prevent pregnancy following unprotected sex or a contraceptive failure if taken within 72 hours. It also provides condoms, birth-control pills and pregnancy testing. [64]

Teen Sex Slave Trade Hits Home

Teen prostitutes, not even old enough to drive, walk the streets of our cities selling their bodies every night. They call it "the life," but what they're forced into is sexual slavery.

"I got sold," says Sara, who asked that ABC hide her face and change her name for this story. "Like I was an animal." Mistreated, lonely and living in a foster home in a rough neighborhood, Sara was lured into "the life" by a man who claimed to love her. She was only 13.[65]

The Truth About Teens Sexting

Sex easily and quickly integrated itself into the digital age; and now the teen trend of "sexting"—where a user sends sexually explicit images or messages via text on a cell phone—has parents struggling for a way to address the situation. "We're seeing 14, 15 and 16-year-olds and up are very commonly sharing naked pictures or sexual pictures of themselves," said Internet safety expert Parry Aftab, of Wired Safety ... There's nothing coy about this 21st century amorous pursuit. Children as young as 12, who aren't sexually active, are sending explicit, provocative and even pornographic images to their peers.[66]

IUDs, Implants Urged For Teen Girls' Birth Control

Teenage girls may prefer the pill, the patch or even wishful thinking, but their doctors should be recommending IUDs or hormonal implants—long-lasting and more effective birth control that you don't have to remember to use every time, the nation's leading gynecologists group said Thursday.

The IUD and implants are safe and nearly 100 percent effective at preventing pregnancy, and should be "first-line recommendations," the American College of Obstetricians and Gynecologists said in updating its guidance for teens.[67]

As individuals and as a nation, we have a monumental decision to make: are we going to turn back—or continue to turn our backs—to God?

March 14, 2011

I had an engagement ring on. The diamond was pretty big. The weird thing is, I was engaged to another woman. Eight days before the wedding, I asked her who was going to pay for the wedding. It just occurred to me that we hadn't discussed it. I suggested we pay for it ourselves because we were older. The conversation felt like it was supposed to be with a man, because I was the bride. She didn't agree with me. She said that traditionally the father of the bride should pay. But I said that I knew my father didn't have the thousands needed for this big event, and that I was over 50 years old and shouldn't be asking for my father to pay, no matter what tradition says. Then she said, "Well, you never know. Maybe he does have some money that you don't know about." I thought about calling off the wedding, feeling that we didn't have all that much in common if we couldn't even agree on that.

Chapter Ten
Standing at the Crossroads

"This is what the Lord says: 'Stop at the crossroads and look around. Ask for the old, godly way, and walk in it. Travel its path, and you will find rest for your souls.' But you reply, 'No, that's not the road we want!'" (Jeremiah 6:16 NLT).

"I think same sex couples should be able to get married." Barack Obama said this in a May 2012 interview with Robin Roberts.[68] A year earlier, the president ordered the Justice Department to stop supporting the Defense of Marriage Act,[69] which defines marriage as the legal union between one man and one woman. Yet in 2008, just four years earlier in an MTV interview, Mr. Obama said, "I believe marriage is between a man and a woman. I am not in favor of gay marriage..."[70]

What caused this seismic reversal in such a short period of time? Politics? Perhaps. But it is no coincidence that this historic move, championed by someone many would argue was at the time the most powerful man in the world, came on the heels of the 40th anniversary of Roe vs. Wade.

The number 40 is Biblically significant. The rains in Noah's day fell for 40 days and nights (Genesis 7:4). Moses was with God on Mount Sinai for 40 days and nights (Exodus 24:18, 34:28). Jesus fasted 40 days and nights (Matthew 4:2) and remained on earth 40 days after

His resurrection (Acts 1:3). And because the Israelites did not believe what God told them about the Promised Land, they spent 40 years in the wilderness, where an entire generation died (Deuteronomy 2:14).

Similarly, because we do not believe what God tells us about life, we have spent 40 years in a spiritual wilderness, where an entire generation has died. *"Remember how the LORD your God led you all the way in the wilderness these forty years, to humble you and to test you in order to know what was in your heart..."* (Deuteronomy 8:2 TNIV). And it is interesting that I am writing this 40 years after my first abortion.

I hadn't thought about it before writing this book, but a full term pregnancy lasts 40 weeks. By interrupting the divinely established union of sperm and egg, the "miracle of life" through abortion on demand, we have shown God what is in our heart, haven't we? It is a pride that says, "I am the boss." A pride that has interrupted another divinely established union: Marriage.

Crossroad: A crucial point where a decision must be made

"And the leaders and officials have led the way in this unfaithfulness" (Ezra 9:2 TNIV).

As we said earlier, the Bible defines marriage as the union between one man and one woman. That is the way marriage has been defined for thousands of years. That is how the majority of people in California voted to define it in 2008, in a state constitutional amendment called Proposition 8. But in 2013, again, during the 40th anniversary year of Roe vs. Wade, our modern-day time of testing, the U.S. Supreme Court followed in President Obama's footsteps and overruled the people's vote, allowing same-sex marriages in that state.[71] And then in June 2015, the Supreme Court redefined marriage in an historic ruling by legalizing same sex marriages nationally.[72] This ruling is on par with the Roe vs. Wade, in that it completely ignores what God tells us about life and living and continues to pridefully proclaim, "we are the boss."

Homosexuality Is Nothing New

"What has been will be again, what has been done will be done again; there is nothing new under the sun" (Ecclesiastes 1:9 TNIV).

Homosexuality has been around forever. It is addressed multiple times in the Bible, and each time as a sin. Just as other sexual acts are addressed as sin. Leviticus 18 lists several: "Do not have sexual relations with your father's wife (v. 8)"; "Do not have sexual relations with your sister (v. 9);" "Do not have sexual relations with your father's sister (v.12)". Then verse 22 says, "Do not lie with a man as one lies with a woman; that is detestable."

"Love the sinner, hate the sin" is a phrase Christians sometimes use to say, "I love you, but I don't always love or agree with what you do." Parents feel this way about their children, and God feels this way about us. Regardless of our belief system, we all feel this way from time to time about people we love. I feel this way toward my own family, as well as toward people I love who are gay, married, and raising children.

As we discussed in Chapter Three, "sin" means falling short (of God's perfection), missing the mark. The practice of homosexuality is a sin, just as is premarital sex and adultery. And although acts like stealing and murder are also sins, the Bible says that sexual immorality, particularly for a Christian, is different because:

"All other sins a man commits are outside his body, but he who sins sexually sins against his own body. Do you not know that your body is a temple of the Holy Spirit, who is in you, whom you have received from God? You are not your own; you were bought at a price. Therefore honor God with your body" (1 Corinthians 6:18-20).

I am as much a sinner as are the people I love who are living a gay lifestyle. I am no better, no worse. The Bible says, "Do not judge, or you too will be judged. For in the same way you judge others, you will be judged, and with the measure you use, it will be measured to you" (Matthew 7:1-2 NIV). Jesus goes on to call those of us who judge hypocrites, because we're not looking at ourselves, at our own sin. In addition, the Bible not only tells us not to judge, but that we should think of others more highly than ourselves (Philippians 2:3). But the point is that the common thread undergirding any sin is pride. It's not so much the sexual act as it is the pride beneath it that says, like Miley Cyrus, "we can do what we want, we can say what we want, we can love who we want, we can kiss who we want, we can live how we want."

Through the prophet Ezekiel, God compares the people of Jerusalem to the Sodomites, telling Jerusalem that they are worse. We often hear about Sodom, how that city was destroyed, and the common belief is because of its sexual depravity. But God is telling the people of Jerusalem:

"Your sister Sodom and her daughters never did what you and your daughters have done. Now this was the sin of your sister Sodom: She and her daughters were arrogant, overfed and unconcerned; they did not help the poor and needy. They were haughty and did detestable things before me. Therefore I did away with them as you have seen" (Ezekiel 16:48-50).

Notice what came before the detestable things: arrogance. The King James Version calls it pride.

Jesus speaks to the people of Capernaum in a similar way:

"And you, Capernaum, will you be lifted to the skies? No, you will go down to the depths. For if the miracles that were performed in you had been performed in Sodom, it would have remained to this day. But I tell you that it will be more bearable for Sodom on the day of judgment than for you" (Matthew 11:23-24).

Jesus is telling his audience that if the people of Sodom had seen God in the flesh, had witnessed His miracles as his audience had, they would have repented. But Sodom did not have this chance, so God will be more merciful on them just as He was on me, because I didn't know that He was real. But even though the people in Capernaum had witnessed Jesus in the flesh, and His miracles, their pride kept them from repentance.

And what about us today? How much worse will it be for us? Neither Sodom or Capernaum had the Bible, the "raw meat" of the Word of God as available and verifiable as it is today. Yet we continue to turn our backs on it and "do what we want."

God Loves Everyone the Same

"God does not show favoritism" (Acts 10:34).

In Acts 10:34-35, after God revealed to Peter that the Jewish law about not associating with Gentiles was wrong, Peter said, "I now realize how true it is that God does not show favoritism but accepts those from every nation **who fear him and do what is right**" (emphasis mine). That means it doesn't matter if we are male, female, gay, straight, transgender or bisexual. God loves us all equally, and will accept us if we fear him and do "what is right." But what is that? It is repentance—a change of mind and heart that recognizes Jesus as Lord. A perfect example is seen at the Cross.

Jesus loved both of the men, also being crucified, on either side of Him. But one repented and one didn't. Luke 23:39-43 (NLT) records this. "One of the criminals hanging beside him scoffed, 'So you're the Messiah, are you? Prove it by saving yourself—and us, too, while you're at it!' But the other criminal protested, 'Don't you fear God even when you are dying? We deserve to die for our evil deeds, but this man hasn't done anything wrong.' Then he said, 'Jesus, remember me when you come into your Kingdom.' And Jesus replied, 'I assure you, today you will be with me in paradise.'"

Who knows what that man did, what he was being crucified for. Maybe he was a rapist or murderer or pedophile. But it didn't matter to God because He knew the man's heart, that he was truly sorry for what he did, and that he truly recognized Jesus for who He was. And that's what brings us into a right relationship with God: repentance. It is what unleashes God's grace—His unmerited favor—on us. It's not about our understanding of being "good" or even stopping what we're doing that we think is bad, although that's a start. It's about our hearts. It's about *wanting* to stop, and *wanting* to do what's right in God's eyes, not our own. My pastor often says that once we submit to God, He makes us "wanna wanna."

We need to come to realize how much we're "missing the mark," how much we're falling short of God's standard, **and then we need to care about it.**

Just Stop It

"Go now and leave your life of sin" (John 8:11).

In the Gospel of John (8:1-11), the religious leaders brought to Jesus a woman who was caught in the act of adultery. The penalty for that crime at that time was stoning to death. "Teacher, this woman was caught in the act of adultery. In the Law Moses commanded us to stone such women. Now what do you say?"

The Bible says that they were trying to trap Jesus by forcing Him to either go against Mosaic Law, for which they could have accused Him, or agreeing with it, which would have gone against what He taught about loving everyone. But Jesus called their bluff. He said, "If any one of you is without sin, let him be the first to throw a stone at her." And the woman's accusers "...began to go away one at a time, the older ones first, until only Jesus was left with the woman still standing there." Jesus then asked her, "Woman, where are they? Has no one condemned you?" "No one, sir," she said. Then He said to her the same thing He says to us today. "Then neither do I condemn you...Go now, and leave your life of sin."

Many people claim that Jesus is silent on the topic of homosexuality, that He never condemned homosexuality or gay marriage. We have to remember that Jesus was God in the flesh, some say, "God with skin." John 1:14 says, "The Word became flesh and made his dwelling among us." So Jesus was the living embodiment of Scripture, the Bible come to life, if you will. And at that time, Scripture, "the Word," was just the Old Testament, which clearly states that acting on homosexual urges is a sin. Therefore, everything Jesus said was true, whether He said it once or a thousand times. And in Mark 10:6-9, Jesus reaffirmed what is stated in Genesis: "But at the beginning of creation God 'made them male and female. For this reason a man will leave his father and mother and be united to his wife, and the two will become one flesh.' So they are no longer two, but one flesh. Therefore what God has joined together, let man not separate."

When Ravi Zacharias was asked at one of his forums whether a person can live a sincere Christian life as a practicing homosexual, he gave this explanation:

> The reason we are against racism is because a person's race is sacred. A person's ethnicity is sacred. You cannot violate it. My race is sacred; your race is sacred; I dare not violate it. The reason we react against the issue of homosexuality the way we do is because sexuality is sacred. You cannot violate it. How do you treat one as sacred and desacrelize (sic) the other? Sex is a sacred gift of God. I can no longer justify an aberration of it in somebody else's life than I can justify my own proclivities to go beyond my marital boundaries.
>
> Every man here who is an able-bodied man will tell you temptation stalks you every day. Does it have anything to do with your love for your spouse? Probably not, because you can

love your spouse with 100% desire to love the person, but the human body reacts to the sight entertained by the imagination and gives you all kinds of false hints that stolen waters are going to be sweeter. They are not. They leave you emptier. So a disposition or a proclivity does not justify expressing that disposition and that proclivity. That goes across the board for all sexuality.

When God created mankind and womankind, it was His plan, not our plan. It is extraordinary what He said. He said, 'It is not good for man to live alone.' Well, man wasn't living alone; God was with him. Why did He say that? He created the mystique and the majesty and the charm and the complimentary nature of womankind in a way that made it possible for her to meet his emotional needs that God, Himself, put only within her outside himself from himself in her in that complementariness. It is a design by God. [73]

But we have taken it upon ourselves to redesign God's plan, much the same way the early Roman Church did:

"For although they knew God, they neither glorified him as God nor gave thanks to him, but their thinking became futile and their foolish hearts were darkened. ... Therefore God gave them over in the sinful desires of their hearts to sexual impurity for the degrading of their bodies with one another. They exchanged the truth of God for a lie and worshipped and served created things rather than the Creator.... Because of this, God gave them over to shameful lusts. Even their women exchanged natural relations for unnatural ones. In the same way the men also abandoned natural relations with women and were inflamed with lust for one

another. Men committed indecent acts with other men, and received in themselves the due penalty for their perversion" (Romans 1:21, 24-27).

And it's not enough for us to have redesigned God's plan. Now we want to mainstream it.

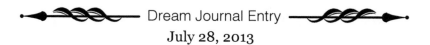

July 28, 2013

There was a family who lived underground, like in a cave. You could only see them if you got on your knees, bent down and looked through this hole. But it was weird. The family was a combination of regular people and cartoon-like characters. I said something like, "That can't be a real family—look at those cartoon characters." But someone else pointed out that they had an address for their house/cave. A number had been assigned, just like everyone else's house. So that supposedly made them legitimate. The person pointed out the number over the cave—360.

Chapter Eleven
Legitimizing Sin

"Woe to those who call evil good and good evil, who put darkness for light and light for darkness, who put bitter for sweet and sweet for bitter" (Isaiah 5:20).

Wikipedia defines a cartoon as "a typically non-realistic drawing or painting intended for satire, caricature, or humor..." And then defines satire as "a genre of literature, and sometimes graphic and performing arts, in which vices, follies, abuses, and shortcomings are held up to ridicule, ideally with the intent of shaming individuals, corporations, government or society itself, into improvement."

I believe the message of this dream, indeed the message of this book, is to "shame us into improvement." To show us how we have come full circle, 360 degrees, from the blueprint laid out for us by God in His Word, the Bible. To confront us with how we are redefining sexuality, marriage, family, and even what constitutes life in order to legitimize aberrant behaviors. And to hopefully and prayerfully turn us back to "the old, godly way" (Jeremiah 6:16 NLT).

Genesis 1:27-28 says, "...male and female he created them. God blessed them and said to them, 'Be fruitful and increase in number...'" This is a clear establishment of the family, just as Genesis 2:24 is a clear establishment of marriage: "That is why a man leaves his father and mother and is united with his wife, and they become one flesh" (GNT). Yet, we continue to twist and distort the truth, until headlines like these make the mainstream news:

Florida Judge Rules Birth Certificate Will List All 3 Gay Parents

A Florida judge has made history by allowing a birth certificate to list as parents a married lesbian couple and a gay man.[74]

Pregnant Man Gives Birth to Girl

Thomas Beatie, the transgender man who made headlines as the so-called "pregnant man," gave birth Sunday to a healthy baby girl, ABC News has learned.[75]

Distorting All That Is Right

"Hear this, you leaders of the house of Jacob...who despise justice and distort all that is right" (Micah 3:9).

The male has testicles that produce sperm. The woman has ovaries that produce eggs. The man's sperm is meant to fertilize the woman's eggs. The only natural way for that to happen is for the man to insert his penis into the woman's vagina to release the sperm. That is what has always been referred to as sexual intercourse. As we said in the previous chapter, God created that process to be sensually pleasurable within the marriage bed, because the process was intended to multiply the human race; to create families. And God wants us to enjoy ourselves!

But President Obama and the Supreme Court have declared that marriage between two men or two women is equivalent to marriage between a man and a woman. They are saying that anal sex between two men or simulated sex between two women is morally equivalent to sex between a man and a woman. Which basically cancels out morality altogether, because there is no longer a moral sexual standard. And anyone who believes there should be a standard is considered "intolerant," "extremist," or "homophobic." But even if you remove God from the equation, scientific evidence points to the fact that sex between two men is not "normal" or equivalent to sex between a man and a woman.

Donald DeMarco, professor emeritus at the University of St. Jerome's College at the University of Waterloo, says in his article, "What Science Tells Us About Same Sex Unions":

> Our immune system, certainly one of the great marvels of nature, equips us with 100 billion (100,000,000,000) immunological receptors. Each of these tiny receptors has the uncanny natural capacity to distinguish the self from the non-self. ...
> Marvelous as nature is, it is never extremist. From a purely immunological point of view (from the standpoint of an all-out defensive strategy), a woman's body would reject the oncoming sperm, recognizing it as a foreign

substance. But this is precisely the point at which nature, we might say, becomes wise. ...

Traveling alongside the sperm in the male's seminal fluid is a mild immunosuppressant. Immunologists refer to it as consisting of "immunoregulatory macromolecules." This immunosuppressant is a chemical signal to the woman's body that allows it to recognize the sperm not as a non-self, but as part of its self. It makes [it] possible ... [for the] woman's immune system to welcome the male sperm as part of her own flesh.

Now ... what happens when sperm is deposited in the rectal area rather than in the vaginal area?

Male sperm, being blissfully unresponsive to political ideologies or cultural trends, go right ahead and behave strictly according to their nature. They penetrate the nucleus of whatever body cell (somatic cell) they might encounter. This fusing, however, does not result in fertilization, the first stage in the life of a new human being, but, as scientists have shown, can and does result in the development of cancerous malignancies....Depositing sperm in the "wrong place" (like pouring motor oil into the gas line), by nature's standards, is courting disaster. Nature, we might add, demands respect. It does not make accommodations to politically based ideologies or individual preferences. From nature's standpoint, there is no equality between heterosexual and male homosexual intercourse. [76]

You can believe that homosexual acts are normal behaviors, but that does not make them so. It's like saying two plus two equals five. You can believe it and say it all you want, but the truth is that two plus two equals four. And the truth is that God calls us to a standard of morality that we have willfully, selfishly, and purposefully abandoned.

In 1997 John McKellar, an openly gay man, founded an organization called HOPE (Homosexuals Opposed to Pride Extremism). Mr. McKellar describes HOPE as "... non-partisan, non-sectarian, unattached to all intents and purposes, and seeks not to indoctrinate or reform, but to comment, criticize and inform..." [77] And he says:

> We're not talking about music, fashion or art. We're talking about an institution whose 4 prohibitions—you can only marry one person at a time, only someone of the opposite sex, never someone beneath a certain age, and not a close blood relative— have been grounded in morality and in law for millennia.... Humankind yearns for these stabilizing factors in our kaleidoscopic world and if we abandon these standards, then everything becomes legal and everything becomes moral. If gay marriages are permitted (a prerogative of the most decadent Roman emperors), why not polygamy? Why not brother and sister or parent and child? [78]

What About the Children?

"These commandments that I give you today are to be upon your hearts. Impress them on your children. Talk about them when you sit at home and when you walk along the road, when you lie down and when you get up" (Deuteronomy 6:6-7).

If we have no moral sexual boundaries, then neither will our children. Little girls or little boys will feel like it's okay to have a same sex boyfriend or girlfriend when they grow up, even if they have no gay tendencies. Anyone who argues this does not know children. They are sponges, absorbing the right or the wrong around them. Now we have the transgender bathroom Federal mandate. [79] That controversy started in 2010 with headlines like these:

School Must Allow 'Transgender" 6th Grader to Use Girls' Bathroom

The Maine Human Rights Commission (HRC) has ruled that a middle school unlawfully discriminated against a "transgender" sixth-grade boy by disallowing the child from entering a girls' bathroom and instead assigning him his own separate bathroom. The matter concerned Orono Middle School's treatment of a child whose parents have insisted has a right to use a girl's bathroom, despite being biologically male, because of his chosen gender identity.[80]

Transgender first-grader wins the right to use girls' restroom

(CNN) — A transgender first-grader who was born a boy but identifies as a girl has won the right to use the girls' restroom at her Colorado school. The Colorado Rights Division ruled in favor of Coy Mathis in her fight against the Fountain-Fort Carson School District.[81]

But what about all of the little girls who will feel uncomfortable sharing a bathroom with a boy? Don't their opinions and feelings count? Does it seem fair to rule in favor of one and against many? And now it seems that not only has marriage been redefined, but so has what we call our children:

Nebraska school suggests teachers avoid calling students boys or girls to be "gender inclusive"

> LINCOLN, Neb. – A Lincoln middle school staffer gave teachers training documents advising them not to use "gendered expressions" by calling students "boys and girls" or "ladies and gentlemen," but to instead use more generic expressions like campers, readers, athletes or even purple penguins to be more "gender inclusive." [82]

Mr. McKellar, of HOPE, further opines:

> To my radical brothers and sisters, sexual orientation is not only a lifestyle, but a religion and a career. It's their whole identity. How absurd and how sad. ...
> As an openly gay male, I have no problem conceding that heterosexuality is and always will be the great human norm. But I'm sick and tired of a media culture that faciley equates homosexuality with heterosexuality and asks no deep questions about human psychology beyond the superficial liberal-vs-conservative, freedom-vs-oppression dichotomy. And I'm sick and tired of the sentimental, feel-good, liberal propaganda that conceals and denies the blatant Roman Empire decadence and

compulsive, tunnel-vision promiscuity of so many gay men's lives.

... You quickly discover that the optimum way to ensure future supporters to your cause and ideology is through the minds of the young. You skillfully master the techniques of invoking sympathy, hiding the truth and presenting a sanitized portrait of gay life.

Introducing kindergarten and grade one students to alternative behaviours and lifestyles is psychological pedophilia. You don't have to engage solely in physical contact to molest a child. You can diddle with their minds and their emotions. And this is exactly what some of my radical brothers and sisters are up to. And this is exactly what a disheartening majority of educators, school trustees and teachers unions endorse.

Spare me the tolerance and compassion bunkum. Just leave the kids alone and let them enjoy their short period of innocence and sexual latency. Then when they approach puberty, balance the pop-culture bombardment with messages of abstinence, discipline and self-control. Don't just assume that all teens are out-of-control hormone factories and that all you can do is shrug your shoulders and throw condoms at them. [83]

We can legalize gay marriage, allow gay adoptions, allow girls to call themselves boys and boys to call themselves girls. But as with abortion, just because something is legal, doesn't mean it's right or moral.

But many ask about gay couples who adopt children who might otherwise live their lives out in orphanages or foster homes. Aren't they doing a good thing? The answer is yes, of course they are. Or gay couples who have children via surrogates or artificial insemination, believing they can provide a good life and loving home for a child. As altruistic as these seem, if at the same time, these couples are actively engaged in homosexual activity, they are not putting God first. Because when Jesus was asked which is the greatest commandment, He said, "Love the Lord your God with all your heart and with all your soul and with all your mind" (Matthew 22:37). And God says that (active) homosexuality is a sin. Just as is adultery, murder, and premarital sex. It's not having homosexual tendencies, it is not "being gay" that is a sin. As Ravi Zacharias said, we all have different desires and proclivities. The sin is acting on them.

Pope Francis exemplified the heart of God when he said, "Who am I to judge a gay person of goodwill who seeks the Lord?"[84] Because God loves that person and desires that person to seek Him. Through the prophet Jeremiah God said, "You will seek me and find me when you seek me with all your heart" (29:13). And when a person does "find" God, they will come to understand what He requires of them. And that understanding will breed a change of mind and heart, a.k.a. repentance. It is what happened to the woman caught in adultery who we discussed earlier. Jesus did not condemn her. He loved her, and said to her, "Go and sin no more" (John 8:11 NLT).

Although the Pope talks about not judging gay people just because they're gay, he does make a judgment about their actions. When speaking against a bill that would allow gay couples in Argentina to adopt children, he said (emphasis mine):

> "The Argentine people will face a situation whose outcome can seriously harm the family," he wrote to the four monasteries in Argentina. "At stake is the identity and survival of the family: father, mother and children. **At stake are the lives of many children who will be discriminated against in advance, and deprived of their human development given by a father and a mother and willed by God. At stake is the total rejection of God's law engraved in our hearts.**" He went on to describe it as a "move of the Father of Lies who seeks to confuse and deceive the children of God" and asked for lawmakers to "not act in error." In John 8:44 the Father of Lies is the devil.[85]

What we need, to keep repeating what the Apostle Paul said, is a transformation of our minds and hearts. And, as Ravi Zacharias says, "All the laws in the world will never change the heart. Only God is big enough for that." [86]

And amazingly, God continues to be merciful and patient with us, giving us chance after chance to stop at the crossroad we've reached and to choose the right path. Yet we pridefully persist in twisting the meaning of "choice" to be anything we want to do, and believe that whatever we want to do will be okay. Like having sex with whoever we want, wherever we want, however we want. And if a baby results from any of those choices, choosing to kill that baby. Even if it is born alive.

Dream Journal Entry
August 15, 2012

*Saw someone performing an abortion. A doctor—
in the house I was in? My house? Knew something
bad was going on—hoping he'd change his mind?
Opened a door to peek/see. A doctor/man bent over
a woman, legs spread, blood between her legs/on
his hands. His hands between her legs full of blood.
I knew he was pulling something/the baby/fetus out
of her. I hated it. Hated he was doing it in my house.
Thinking/hoping he'd realize how awful it was and
want to stop doing it. But thought about the money,
that that may have been his incentive.*

Chapter Twelve
Confronting Choice

"...I have set before you life and death, blessings and curses. Now choose life, so that you and your children may live..." (Deuteronomy 30:19).

Abortion, to most people, means the termination of a pregnancy at such an early stage that the word, "baby" isn't even considered. It's the mindset I held when I had my abortions.

But the reality of where that mindset leads is something no one, not even the most staunch "pro-choice" advocates, want to know or admit. That's why the horrific acts of one late-term abortionist was hidden from the mainstream news, until it no longer could be. A cautionary note to the reader is warranted here. What follows are graphic descriptions of one doctor's late-term abortion practices.

In April of 2013, Kermit Gosnell, a late-term abortionist, was brought into the living rooms of America. Although Mr. Gosnell had been indicted by a grand jury in 2011 on eight counts of murder and 24 felony counts of illegal abortions beyond the 24-week limit, the case was not covered in the media for over two years, until his actual trial. Why? Because it's hard to read things like this, uncovered in Kirstin Powers' USA Today article on April 11, 2013.

Infant beheadings. Severed baby feet in jars. A child screaming after it was delivered alive during an abortion procedure. Haven't heard about these sickening accusations? It's not your fault. Since the murder trial of Pennsylvania abortion doctor Kermit Gosnell began March 18, there has been precious little coverage of the case that should be on every news show and front page. The revolting revelations of Gosnell's former staff, who have been testifying to what they witnessed and did during late-term abortions, should shock anyone with a heart. [87]

"Then confront them with their detestable practices" (Ezekiel 23:36).

Ms. Powers was doing exactly what God told Ezekiel to do when addressing the northern and southern kingdoms of Israel, who were engaging in all forms of apostasy, idolatry, and immorality, including child sacrifice. The grand jury report that indicted Gosnell goes on to confront these "detestable practices" in even more detail. The facts speak better and stronger than I ever could, so the balance of this chapter is mainly from the introduction of that report (any emphasis mine):

> This case is about a doctor who killed babies and endangered women. What we mean is that he regularly and illegally delivered live, viable, babies in the third trimester of pregnancy—and then murdered these newborns by severing their spinal cords with scissors. The medical practice by which he

carried out this business was a filthy fraud in which he overdosed his patients with dangerous drugs, spread venereal disease among them with infected instruments, perforated their wombs and bowels—and, on at least two occasions, caused their deaths. **Over the years, many people came to know that something was going on here. But no one put a stop to it.** [88]

Isn't it hard to believe that anyone knew about this and didn't report it? The report continues:

The "Women's Medical Society." That was the impressive-sounding name of the clinic operated in West Philadelphia, at 38th and Lancaster, by Kermit B. Gosnell, M.D. Gosnell seemed impressive as well. A child of the neighborhood, Gosnell spent almost four decades running this clinic, giving back—so it appeared—to the community in which he continued to live and work. But the truth was something very different, and evident to anyone who stepped inside. The clinic reeked of animal urine, courtesy of the cats that were allowed to roam (and defecate) freely. Furniture and blankets were stained with blood. Instruments were not properly sterilized. Disposable medical supplies were not disposed of; they were reused, over and over again. Medical equipment – such as the defibrillator, the EKG, the pulse oximeter, the blood pressure cuff – was generally broken; even when it worked, it wasn't used. The emergency exit was padlocked shut. **And scattered throughout, in cabinets, in the basement, in a freezer, in jars and bags and plastic jugs, were fetal remains. It was a baby charnel house.**" [89]

"This is what the LORD says: "For three sins of Ammon, even for four, I will not turn back [my wrath]. Because he ripped open the pregnant women of Gilead in order to extend his borders" (Amos 1:13).

Here is one example of what happened to a baby the report calls, "Baby Boy A."

> One such baby was a boy born in July 2008 to [a] 17-year-old we will call "Sue." Sue first met Gosnell at the Atlantic Women's Medical Services, an abortion clinic in Wilmington, Delaware, where Gosnell worked one day a week. The girl was accompanied by her great aunt, who had agreed to pay for the procedure, and who testified before the Grand Jury. After an ultrasound was performed on Sue, Gosnell told the aunt that the girl's pregnancy was further along than she had originally told him, and that, therefore, the procedure would cost more than the $1,500 that had been agreed upon; it would now cost $2,500. (Gosnell normally charged $1,625 for 23-24 week abortions.) The aunt paid Gosnell in cash at the Delaware clinic. He inserted laminaria, gave Sue pills to begin labor, and instructed her to be at the Women's Medical Center in Philadelphia at 9:00 the next morning. Sue arrived with her aunt at 9:00 a.m. and did not leave the clinic until almost 11:00 that night. An ultrasound conducted by Kareema Cross recorded a gestational age of 29.4 weeks. Cross testified that the girl appeared to be seven or eight months pregnant. Cross said that, during 13-plus hours, the girl was given a large amount of Cytotec to induce labor and delivery.
>
> Sue complained of pain and was heavily sedated. According to Cross, the girl was left to labor for hours and hours. Eventually, she

gave birth to a large baby boy. Cross estimated that the baby was 18 to 19 inches long. She said he was nearly the size of her own six pound, six ounce, newborn daughter. After the baby was expelled, Cross noticed that he was breathing, though not for long. After about 10 to 20 seconds, while the mother was asleep, 'the doctor just slit the neck,' said Cross. Gosnell put the boy's body in a shoebox. Cross described the baby as so big that his feet and arms hung out over the sides of the container. Cross said that she saw the baby move after his neck was cut, and after the doctor placed it in the shoebox. Gosnell told her, "it's the baby's reflexes. It's not really moving."

The neonatologist testified that what Gosnell told his people was absolutely false. If a baby moves, it is alive. Equally troubling, it feels a 'tremendous amount of pain' when its spinal cord is severed. So, the fact that Baby Boy A continued to move after his spinal cord was cut with scissors means that he did not die instantly. Maybe the cord was not completely severed. In any case, his few moments of life were spent in excruciating pain. Cross was not the only one startled by the size and maturity of Baby Boy A. Adrienne Moton and Ashley Baldwin, along with Cross, took photographs because they knew this was a baby that could and should have lived. Cross explained:

Q. Why did you all take a photograph of this baby?

A. Because it was big and it was wrong and we knew it. We knew something was wrong. I'm not sure who took the picture first, but when we seen this baby, it was – it was a shock to us because I never seen a baby that big that he had done. So it was – I knew something was wrong because everything, like you can see everything, the hair, eyes, everything. And I never seen for any other procedure that he did, I never seen any like that.

The neonatologist viewed a photograph of Baby Boy A. Based on the baby's size, hairline, muscle mass, subcutaneous tissue, well-developed scrotum, and other characteristics, the doctor opined that the boy was at least 32 weeks, if not more, in gestational age.

Gosnell simply noted the baby boy's size by joking, as he often did after delivering a large baby. According to Cross, the doctor said: "This baby is big enough to walk around with me or walk me to the bus stop." [90]

Here is a photo from the grand jury report (pg 102, in color):

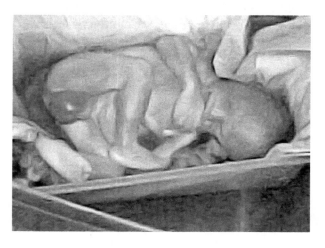

"For all the people had been weeping as they listened to the words of the Law" (Nehemiah 8:9).

If you have become squeamish, that's a good sign. It means you have a conscience. Which is what we, as a nation, need to reclaim.

But if you think (and hope) that Gosnell is an anomaly, sadly, he's not. There is an organization called "Live Action," which has documented at least eight other late-term abortion clinics/practitioners. We don't need any more graphic detail in this chapter, but unfortunately there is plenty on this website: http://www.liveaction.org/inhuman/.

Here is how one clinic describes the procedure for a pregnancy of 20 weeks or more on their website (emphasis mine):

> If you are 20 weeks pregnant or more by ultrasound, the physician will also administer a medication called digoxin on the first day of your abortion procedure. **Digoxin is used to stop a fetal heart beat.** When the dilation of your cervix is complete you will be taken to the operating room, and an anesthesiologist will administer anesthesia. The surgery will begin when the physician inserts a speculum into your vagina in order to view your cervix. If necessary, the physician will then dilate (open) your cervix more by inserting thin, metal rods, one by one, into the opening of the cervix. These rods, called dilators, gradually increase in width. The physician will then use surgical instruments and vacuum aspiration (suction) **to remove your pregnancy**. The surgery usually takes approximately 10 to 20 minutes. After your surgery, you will be monitored in our recovery room until you are medically cleared to go home, usually 45 minutes. [91]

Compared to the Gosnell grand jury report, this description sounds very sanitized, doesn't it? What it describes being removed is the woman's "pregnancy," not her baby, even though the "pregnancy" has a heartbeat. But because the Gosnell case was publicized, we now know it is a baby, and it has been a baby all along. It's just gotten bigger. Yet, under the deceptive guise of "choice" and "reproductive rights," we have come to allow that baby (and 57 million others including mine) to be ripped to shreds by surgical instruments and we administer poison to stop its heartbeat.

When we redefine what God says about life and when it begins so that we can satisfy and justify what we want to do, it seems perfectly in order to redefine every other moral code and tenet. So if we've reached the point where life itself doesn't matter, then it follows that nothing else will matter either.

Yet, there is hope. There is evidence that our national conscience is embedded with God's moral law. Because even though everything we have read in this chapter is true; even though abortion on demand is the law of the land and there are more Gosnells out there:

A pack of cigarettes says, "smoking during pregnancy can harm your baby."[92] The warning does not say "pregnancy," "fetus," or "embryo." It says, "baby."

A bottle of liquor says, "According to the Surgeon General, women should not drink alcoholic beverages during pregnancy because of the risk of birth defects."[93]

Birth defects to who? The "nonperson" inside the mother? Both these warnings are clearly directed at the baby in the womb.

And we have legislation to delay a death sentence on a pregnant woman until after she delivers her baby.[94]

If we, as a nation, really believed that a baby in the womb is just a blob of tissue, or a "nonperson," why would we have these federally mandated warnings and laws?

If I asked you if crack cocaine or rape should be made legal just because people are going to do it anyway, would you say yes? Yet this is the argument that is made for making and keeping abortion legal.

If I asked you if it should be legal for a man to have two wives because he loves them equally, what would you say? Yet one of the arguments for same sex marriage is that people should be allowed to marry who they love.

If I asked you if it's okay to kill a baby born alive as the result of a late-term abortion, what would you say? Yet Kermit Gosnell pled not guilty to the charges of murder against him.

We cannot continue to have it both ways. We must confront our choices and the sea of depravity they have led to. We must begin to navigate according to the innate compass of our God-given conscience. But first we need to recognize that we have one.

 Dream Journal Entry
January 17, 2011

I was part of a plot to assassinate people. Another guy involved. We were going to kill/have people killed, and then pretend to solve the murders. We were being "duplicitous." It was an elaborate scheme. But then my conscience started bothering me and I told the guy something like, "Look, I'm a Christian, and I just can't do this/go through with this." He was disappointed, because we had spent a lot of time preparing and planning.

Chapter Thirteen
Reclaiming Conscience

"For I know my transgressions, and my sin is always before me" (Psalm 51:3).

The definition of duplicity is, "the belying of one's true intentions by deceptive words or action." The devil is the king of duplicity. Serial killers are perfect examples of duplicitous personalities. They charm their victims with the intent of getting them into a vulnerable position so that they can kill them. Serial killers have no sense of conscience or remorse, which is what separates them from most of us.

King David, a Biblical icon, was duplicitous in his adulterous affair with Bathsheba. When he found out she was pregnant, he called her husband, Uriah, off the battle field so that he would sleep with her and then the baby would appear to be Uriah's. But Uriah insisted on sleeping outside of his house on the doormat, in comradeship with his soldiers who were still on the battlefield. So David arranged to have him killed when he returned to battle, and then took Bathsheba as another of his wives. (Please note that although in biblical times it was customary for a king to have multiple wives, that did not mean that God approved it, and negative consequences always resulted. Deuteronomy 17:17 says this about appointing a king, "He must not take many wives, or his heart will be led astray."

God's original plan, as discussed earlier, is for marriage to be between one man and one woman).

In His mercy, God sent the prophet, Nathan, to King David. Nathan told a story about two men. One who had hundreds of cattle and lambs and another who had only one little ewe lamb. The first man was expecting company and instead of using one of his many stock, he stole the other man's only little lamb. David responded, "That man should die!" And Nathan said, "That man is you."

The verse that opens this chapter is from the Psalm where David is truly repenting before God because of what he did with Bathsheba and Uriah. He also says, "Have mercy on me, O God, according to your unfailing love; according to your great compassion blot out my transgressions. Wash away all my iniquity and cleanse me from my sin" (verse 1-2). And that is why King David is called, "a man after God's own heart." Because David had a conscience, realized the error of his ways, and truly repented.

But even though David repented, there were consequences for what he had done. The child conceived with Bathsheba died, and David's son, Absalom, betrayed him. And so it will be with us, if we do not repent, if we do not reclaim our conscience. There will be consequences. If not in this life, then the next. The Bible says, "For we must all appear before the judgment seat of Christ, so that each of us may receive what is due us for the things done while in the body, whether good or bad" (2 Corinthians 5:10).

King David did not realize his sin until it was pointed out to him. Had God not, in His mercy, sent Nathan to David, he may have gone on with his life, doing whatever he wanted to. But God knew David's heart, just like He knows ours. And that is why God is having me write this book. In His mercy, God gave me the dream about the baby in the bottle. Without it, I don't know that I ever would have realized the depth of what I did to those children in my womb. And just as I was confronted with my transgressions, God wants to point out ours, to confront our duplicitous tendencies, and to revive our collective conscience.

Out of the Mouths of Babes

"Let the little children come to me, and do not hinder them, for the kingdom of God belongs to such as these" (Luke 18:16).

"What's wrong, sweetie?"

My daughter, Sarah, became potty trained shortly before she started preschool. I still monitored her bathroom routine. One day I noticed her little brow was furrowed and her right fist was tightly clenched.

She looked down and opened her hand. A tiny wooden "Little Person" toy rested in her palm.

"Where did you get that?"

"From school."

"Did the teacher tell you it was okay to take that home?"

Still looking down, she shook her head.

"Then why did you take it?"

"Chelsea told me to do it. She said it was okay."

But I told her it wasn't okay, that it was stealing, and that it was wrong.

She kicked her little legs against the toilet base, her voice anguished. "I wish I never did it. I wish I never did it."

I knew that her heart was genuinely troubled, that she was truly remorseful. When I took her to school the next day, we returned the toy and I had her apologize to her teacher.

Haven't all of us, at one time or another, felt that pang of conscience, that guilt, that inner knowing that what we did or what we were doing was wrong? It pains me to remember that this is what I felt after aborting what could have been Sarah's sister or brother. But how did a three year old know to have that much remorse? I'd probably told her somewhere in her short life that stealing was wrong, but I couldn't remember having had that conversation.

Could it be that she was innately created with that knowledge? Remember the woman with the double pregnancy in Chapter Six? She said, "I just couldn't sleep at night knowing that I terminated my daughter's perfectly healthy twin brother." She probably lives every day saying, "I wish I never did it." And why? Again, the Apostle Paul:

"When outsiders who have never heard of God's law follow it more or less by instinct, they confirm its truth by their

144

obedience. *They show that God's law is not something alien, imposed on us from without, but woven into the very fabric of our creation. There is something deep within them that echoes God's yes and no, right and wrong...*" (Romans 2:14-15, MSG, emphasis mine).

The Apostle Paul tried to explain this inner struggle to the Romans:

"*For I have the desire to do what is good, but I cannot carry it out. For what I do is not the good I want to do; no, the evil I do not want to do—this I keep on doing...So I find this law at work: When I want to do good, evil is right there with me. For in my inner being, I delight in God's law; but I see another law at work in the members of my body, waging war against the law of my mind and making me a prisoner of the law of sin at work within my members...*" And then he says, "*Who will rescue me from this body of death? Thanks be to God—through Jesus Christ our Lord*" (Romans 7:18-19, 21-23, 24-25).

The Gosnell case shows us just how far we have strayed from knowing and applying right from wrong. It is what happens when God-given moral principles are abandoned and redefined. It is why we have two diametrically opposed "Christian" reviews of "Wolf of Wall Street." It is why our government puts warnings on cigarettes and alcohol about harm to a baby in the womb, yet legalizes destruction of that same baby through abortion on demand. We have become a morally schizophrenic society.

What Makes Us Feel Bad?

"Against you, you only, have I sinned and done what is evil in your sight" (Psalm 51:4).

When I was eighteen, I took a road trip with my parents and sister to Florida. I'd just gotten my license, so we shared the driving. One night when I was driving on Interstate 95 an unmistakable thump bounced the tires of the 65 Ford. We all knew I'd run over an animal, probably a cat or a rabbit. A pained silence filled the car, as we were a family of animal lovers. But I was the one who had been driving, so I felt the most remorseful.

Six years later when I had my first abortion, though I did feel a sense of remorse, it wasn't even close to what I felt when I ran over that cat or rabbit.

And what happens when we see a dead squirrel, deer or other wildlife on the side of the road? We're pierced with compassion, aren't we? Many of us don't even want to kill bugs or spiders—we have more compassion for them than we do the baby in the womb.

Really, think about it. A rabbit. A squirrel. A bug. A baby. In your heart of hearts, which would you feel worse about killing? Yet, as we said in Chapter Six, we continue to be "sung to sleep by philosophies that save the trees and kill the children."

Former Surgeon General, C. Everett Koop (no relation to me), attempts to define when life begins in his book, *Whatever Happened to the Human Race?*

> We now know when life begins because the test-tube baby proves that life begins with conception. What do you have in the dish? An egg and a sperm. What do you add to it to get a baby? Nothing." Though it is wee, it is still a real person, just as a crumb of bread is still real bread. No one who has been given the gift of life should dare despise the day of small beginnings. Have we forgotten so quickly that we were once as small? [95]

In his speech to the Vatican on January 13, 2014, Pope Francis called our culture a "throwaway society," where "...what is thrown away is not only food and dispensable objects, but often human beings themselves, who are discarded as 'unnecessary'. For example, it is frightful even to think there are children, victims of abortion, who will never see the light of day." [96]

Yes, frightful "even to think" about it. But that is precisely the message of this book. Not only to think about it, but to be confronted with it. We have become so estranged from God that we have reached the point where we are, literally, throwing life away.

In her book, *Abandoned: the Untold Story of the Abortion Wars*, Monica Miller recounts her days as a pro-life activist. She writes:

> On the dock were three green dumpsters. Several heavy-duty cardboard barrels were stacked along the back wall. We began to walk slowly down the ramp. I could see dozens and dozens of boxes strewn haphazardly about the dock. As we approached

I felt a cold numbness stealing over me. When we reached the loading dock I knelt by a stack of boxes to examine them more closely. Pulling back the flaps of one of the boxes, I saw that it was filled to the top with the bodies of aborted babies. There were literally hundreds of them, all packed in the familiar Whirl-Paks and specimen jars. Each box on the dock was similarly filled with fetal remains. The cardboard barrels also contained Whirl-Paks, mixed in with waste and debris. I was struck by the realization that all of these fetal children had been alive only a few short days ago. Now they lay dead and abandoned, cut from their mothers' wombs, cut from the human race: corpses of fetal bodies stacked on a loading dock inside an industrial park in boxes marked "for disposal. [97]

Babies in bottles thrown in the trash. 57 million of them. How can such a horrific wrong be righted?

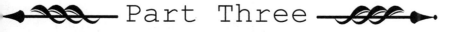

Part Three
About Him

"But do not forget this one thing, dear friends:
With the Lord a day is like a thousand years,
and a thousand years are like a day.
The Lord is not slow in keeping his promise,
as some understand slowness.
He is patient with you,
not wanting anyone to perish,
but everyone to come to repentance."

— 2 Peter 3:8-9

 Dream Journal Entry
April 15, 2012

I was standing in front of shelves that were piled high with boxes of equipment. The boxes were long and rectangular, packaged for sale in a black and white design. I wasn't sure what they were. Then I was sitting down and a man came over to me and handed me one of the boxes. I asked what it was, and he said, "a wireless router." I was confused, asked him why he was giving it to me, and he said, "Because the manufacturer is dead." And I knew that because the person had died, all of his stuff was now free.

Chapter Fourteen
Offering Direction

"I am the way and the truth and the life. No one comes to the Father except through me" (John 14:6).

At first I didn't understand what that dream was about—a wireless router of all things. But as I was recording the dream, as soon as I wrote the word "free," Jesus came to mind.

A Technological Parable

"Why do you speak to the people in parables?" (Matthew 13:10)

Parables are stories from everyday life that relate and illustrate spiritual truths. I read somewhere that the language of the Holy Spirit is the language of the parable. If Jesus were speaking to farmers, He would talk about seeds and growing crops. If He were addressing shepherds, He would use sheep. I believe the dream that opens this chapter is meant to be such a parable for today.

Not too long ago, our computers had to be "hard wired," physically connected by an ethernet cable to a modem in order to access the internet. That cable restricted our connection—without it there was no access. But today we have wireless routers that allow our computers to access the internet without any cables or wires. Most of us have wireless routers in our homes. That's how I'm writing this and maybe how you're reading it. These devices allow portability and give us independence. We can cook dinner while following a recipe on our laptop, iPad, or iPhone without wires and cables getting in the way of our onions and garlic.

In the Old Testament, only repeated animal sacrifices, primarily lambs and goats, could atone for peoples' sin and allow communion with God. Access to God was "hard wired," if you will, to that sacrificial law. Leviticus 17:11 says, "For the life of a creature is in the blood, and I have given it to you to make atonement for yourselves on the altar; it is the blood that makes atonement for one's life."

But in the New Testament, Jesus' death was the ultimate, the once-for-all human sacrifice, giving us direct access to God the Father. That's why Jesus is called, "the Lamb of God." He said, "For this is my blood of the new testament, which is shed for many for the remission of sins" (Matthew 26:28 KJV). Jesus was explaining a previous statement that He made when He said, "Do not think that I have come to abolish the Law or the Prophets; I have not come to abolish them but to fulfill them" (Matthew 5:17-20).

In the same way that wireless routers allow us to access the internet, so Jesus' death on the Cross allows us access to God. Because Jesus is "the manufacturer": "Through him all things were made; without him nothing was made that has been made" (John 1:3). And "God so loved the world that he gave his only begotten son that whoever believes in him shall not perish but have eternal life" (John 3:16 NASB). What that means is God loves us so much that He sent Jesus, His Son, the God-in-the-flesh man that no one can fully comprehend, to die in our place. He was the sacrifice for our sins, so that we can, through Jesus, have a relationship with Almighty God, the Father of the universe. Wild, isn't it? Because Jesus, the manufacturer, died, all of His "stuff" (freedom, salvation, eternal life) is free for anyone who believes in Him.

But we have a problem believing that, believing in Jesus as the Son of God who sacrificed Himself for us and then was raised from the dead. Because the whole thing seems so far-fetched, so far out. But doesn't it seem just as far out, just as far-fetched, to be able to communicate with, even see, someone across the globe on a tiny device held in your hand?

And just as we don't see any wires connecting our computers, iPads or iPhones to the internet and so don't think about what is enabling that connection (unless something goes wrong), we don't see how Jesus connects us to God. So let's find out.

155

What is Salvation?

"...if you confess with your mouth, "Jesus is Lord," and believe in your heart that God raised him from the dead, you will be saved. For it is with your heart that you believe and are justified, and it is with your mouth that you confess and are saved" (Romans 10:9-10).

Webster's dictionary defines salvation as, "the saving of a person from sin or its consequences esp. in the life after death; the saving from danger, difficulty or evil; something that saves."

So Jesus offers to "save" us from the consequences of our "sin" (which, remember, runs the gamut from telling a lie to committing murder), **especially** "in the life after death." The dictionary states that there **is** life after death, and many people, maybe even you, have more confidence in the dictionary than in the Bible.

So let's assume two things: One, that there is life after death. And two, that what we do here on earth has consequences in that afterlife. That means that there must be someone who makes a judgment on what those consequences will be, much like in a courtroom where a suspect is determined, by a judge, to be either guilty or not guilty. The guilty person goes to jail; the not guilty person is set free.

When we believe in and receive the free gift of salvation that Jesus died to give us (as explained in Romans 10:9-10 above), we will be able to stand before Almighty God, the "judge" and be declared "not guilty." Because God will see in us, covering us, the blood of His son, Jesus, who sacrificed Himself in our place. In the New Testament, The Apostle Paul references Leviticus 17:11 when he says, "In fact, the law requires that nearly everything be cleansed with blood, and without the shedding of blood there is no forgiveness" (Hebrews 9:22). So because Christ shed His blood for us, in place of us, we will not be judged for any of the things we did. When we leave our physical bodies, we will be with God, in heaven, in a glorious, fabulous place that "no eye has seen, no ear has heard, no mind has conceived..." (1 Corinthians 2:9).

But the wonderful part about salvation is that we can live here on earth knowing all of this, and because we know the truth (Jesus said He **is** the truth), we can live in freedom, through Him, before we die. We can ask the Spirit of God to help us overcome our imperfections (a.k.a. sins), and live a guilt-free, joy-filled life. Because there is no condemnation in Christ Jesus (Romans 8:1). And when the Son sets you free you are free indeed (John 8:36).

Again, we come back to the subject of this book: choice. Jesus said, "I am the way, the truth and the life. No one comes to the Father except through me" (John 14:6). Jesus says He is "the" way, not one of many. It is a statement I had a lot of trouble with, as do many others. Because we don't like that exclusivity. It seems too narrow, too limiting. After all, what about all the people who believe something else? What about the millions of Buddhists or Muslims who think they are on the path to God?

I heard Greg Laurie, renowned pastor and evangelist, speak to this once. And I was surprised when he said that he agrees that all these people are, in fact, on the path to God, that there really are "many ways up the mountain." He pointed out that the Bible says in Hebrews 9:27 that, "...man is destined to die once, and after that to face judgment..." So no matter which path we take, we will, in fact, at the end of our lives, find and face Almighty God. But Mr. Laurie then pointed out that God the Father will ask us something like, "What did you do about my Son, Jesus?" Where we spend eternity will depend on how we answer that question now.

This is why Jesus says in Matthew 28:19-20: "Therefore go and make disciples of all nations, baptizing them in the name of the Father and of the Son and of the Holy Spirit, and teaching them to obey everything I have commanded you." This directive is known as "the great commission." Jesus told His disciples to "spread the word," to tell people about Him. It is what all Christians are supposed to do. It is what I am doing here. Then it's up to each individual to, again, choose. But what that choice involves is "obeying," which we don't want to do.

We want to either define God in our own way or ignore Him completely, so that we can be the boss. But what if Jesus is who He claimed to be? And there is a mound of

158

evidence pointing to the fact that He is. Do we really want to take the chance of going the wrong way? That is exactly what I had to come to terms with.

Is Jesus Really God?

"If you knew me, you would know my father also" (John 8:19).

These are historical facts: Jesus Christ walked the earth, claimed to be God, predicted His death, performed miracles, died by crucifixion, and was buried in a tomb which was found empty three days later. The Bible says Jesus was subsequently seen by over 500 people. He was, literally, and as He prophesied many times, raised from the dead. All but one of His disciples (Judas Iscariot, who betrayed Jesus, then committed suicide) were brutally murdered because they would not deny or renounce Jesus' divinity. Would you die for a lie?

Before my brother's death, I didn't have a clue about any of this. About Jesus, God, or anything faith or religious based. What I did have, though, was a fascination with anything supernatural. To me, that meant ghosts, ouija boards, and psychics. I didn't know that the definition of supernatural (in Webster's Dictionary) includes *divinity*: "of or relating to phenomena beyond or outside of nature; especially relating to or attributed to a divinity, ghost or devil." My awareness of the supernatural included only the dark, not the light. But as I began reading the Bible and learning about Jesus, I realized that being raised from the dead is about as supernatural as you can get. As is eternity, the concept of living forever. And the Bible says that God has "...planted eternity in the human heart" (Ecclesiastes 3:11 NLT).

Think about a longing or a nostalgic yearning that you sometimes have. Maybe for someone who has died, maybe for a time past, like when you were younger, or when your children were small. That ache, that wistful longing for what you feel you will never have again has been "planted" in your heart by your Creator. Because you and I were made to live forever (that's what God intended with Adam and Eve). And so coming to grips with time, how quickly it passes, and its inevitable consequence—death—is difficult and seems unnatural.

Without a knowledge of God, those yearnings and that grief can bring us to points of hopelessness and despair. It is the point that too many of us have reached searching for meaning, trying to fill the yearning with drugs or alcohol. But when we realize who God is—Jesus Christ—and surrender our lives to Him, we know we will live forever. Because Jesus gives us hope, eternal hope. "In My Father's house are many mansions: if it were not so, I would have told you. I go to prepare a place for you" (John 14:2 KJV). It is what Colossians 1:27 means: "Christ in you, the hope of glory." And what St. Augustine meant when he said, "... you have made us and drawn us to yourself, and our heart is unquiet until it rests in you."[98]

Is the Bible Really True?

"Were not our hearts burning within us while he talked with us on the road and opened the Scriptures to us?" (Luke 24:32).

As I said earlier, before reading *The Purpose Driven Life,* I had never been exposed to the Bible. I had always thought of it as a book found in hotel night stands that helped weak people feel stronger. I had the preconceived notion that it was filled with fairy-tale-like stories used to entertain children in Sunday Schools. And I would bet that a good portion of the population, probably even many people reading this book, have a similar belief. I was living the words of the prophet Hosea: "My people are destroyed from lack of knowledge" (4:6).

God's purpose for me writing this is not to convince you of the Bible's accuracy, but rather to convict your heart with its truth. Jesus tells us that He IS the truth: "I am the way, the truth and the life" (John 4:16). The Apostle John tells us, "In the beginning was the Word, and the Word was with God, and the Word was God. He was with God in the beginning. Through him all things were made; without him nothing was made that has been made. In him was life, and that life was the light of men. The light shines in the darkness, but the darkness has not understood it.... He was in the world, and though the world was made through him, the world did not recognize him.... The Word became flesh and made his dwelling among us..." (John 1: 1-5, 10, 14).

So we have Jesus telling us that He's the Truth, and John telling us that the Word (what we now call the Bible, but at the time was just the Old Testament) WAS God and that Jesus is the Word. So, Jesus is the Bible, the Living Word. When we read the Bible, we discover who Jesus/God is. I've heard the Bible described as God's "Facebook," that if we want to see God's face, we need to read His Book. Imagine how different the world would be if we spent as much time in God's Word as we do in social media.

If you want to find out about the historical and factual accuracy of the Bible, there is a plethora of information available. But here are a few indisputable facts. The Bible consists of 66 books written by 40 different authors over 1500 years in three different languages on three different continents. This collection of books shares a common storyline—the creation, fall, and redemption of God's people; a common theme—God's universal love for all of humanity; and a common message—salvation is available to all who repent of their sins and commit to following Jesus with all of their heart, soul, mind, and strength.

One of the most compelling archeological findings supporting the Old Testament was the discovery of the Dead Sea Scrolls in 1948. One of the lengthiest scrolls found was that of the prophet Isaiah. This scroll was over one thousand years old and when it was translated, matched almost exactly what we have today in its 66 chapters. Many critics of the Bible claim that it can't be accurate, that it's been changed over the years because of all the different translations. This discovery disproves that claim.

Another account as to why the Bible, particularly the New Testament, is an accurate, historical document comes from Ron Rhodes of Reasoning From Scripture Ministries:

> By comparing the manuscript support for the Bible with manuscript support for other ancient documents and books, it becomes overwhelmingly clear that no other ancient piece of literature can stand up to the Bible. Manuscript support for the Bible is unparalleled! There are more [New Testament] manuscripts copied with greater accuracy and earlier dating than for any secular classic from antiquity.
>
> Rene Pache adds, "The historical books of antiquity have a documentation infinitely less solid."
>
> Dr. Benjamin Warfield concludes, "If we compare the present state of the text of the New Testament with that of no matter what other ancient work, we must...declare it marvelously exact."
>
> Norman Geisler makes several key observations for our consideration:
>
> "No other book is even a close second to the Bible on either the number or early dating of the copies. The average secular work from antiquity survives on only a handful of manuscripts; the New Testament boasts thousands. The average gap between the original composition and the earliest copy is over 1,000 years for other books.
>
> "The New Testament, however, has a fragment within one generation from its original composition, whole books within about 100 years from the time of the

autograph [original manuscript], most of the New Testament in less than 200 years, and the entire New Testament within 250 years from the date of its completion.

"The degree of accuracy of the copies is greater for the New Testament than for other books that can be compared. Most books do not survive with enough manuscripts that make comparison possible."

From this documentary evidence, then, it is clear that the New Testament writings are superior to comparable ancient writings. [99]

So if it's all true; if Jesus is really the Son of God; if He died for us, shouldn't we be taking what He did and what He says seriously? Think about it—when push came to shove, would you die for someone else? The Bible says that's just what God did for us. "Greater love has no one than this: to lay down one's life for one's friends" (John 15:13 TNIV). If you were crossing a busy street, and someone ran up and pulled you out of the way of a speeding car, sacrificing their own life in the process, wouldn't you feel indebted to that person? Jesus pulled us out of the way of that speeding car, and here is what He is asking us to do:

"Come to me, all you who are weary and burdened, and I will give you rest. Take my yoke upon you and learn from me, for I am gentle and humble in heart, and you will find rest for your souls. For my yoke is easy and my burden is light" (Matthew 11:28-30).

Doesn't this seem like an unbelievably gracious exchange? Yet we continue to refuse the offer, insisting on holding on to our own heavy yokes instead.

It's Not About Us

"Focusing on self is the opposite of focusing on God" (Romans 8:7 MSG).

The first four words in *The Purpose Driven Life* are, "It's not about you." Rick Warren goes on to say, "Contrary to what many popular books, movies and seminars tell you, you won't discover your life's meaning by looking within yourself.... You didn't create yourself, so there's no way you can tell yourself what you were created for. ... Many people try to use God for their own self-actualization, but that is a reversal of nature and is doomed to failure" (pg. 18). The Message version of the Bible puts it this way:

"Those who think they can do it on their own end up obsessed with measuring their own moral muscle but never get around to exercising it in real life. Those who trust God's action in them find that God's Spirit is in them—living and breathing God! Obsession with self in these matters is a dead end; attention to God leads us out into the open, into a spacious, free life. Focusing on the self is the opposite of focusing on God. Anyone completely absorbed in self ignores God, ends up thinking more about self than God. That person ignores who God is and what he is doing. And God isn't pleased at being ignored" (Romans 8:5-8 MSG).

Yet many New Age and eastern spiritual philosophies follow this belief of going within ourselves to find God. "Christians" who buy into the New Age beliefs incorrectly use, take out of context, and interpret Luke 17:21 as a confirmation of the basis of their teachings. The end of that verse, in the NIV translation, says, "...the kingdom of God is within you." But the word "within" in Greek, the original language of the Bible, means "in the midst of."[100] Jesus was responding to the Pharisees who asked Him when the kingdom of God was going to come. Jesus responded, "The kingdom of God does not come with your careful observation, nor will people say, 'Here it is,' or 'There it is,' because the kingdom of God is within you" (verses 19-21).

The people Jesus was addressing wanted to kill Him. He would not be telling them that God was in their hearts. Indeed, in John 8:44, Jesus tells the same people, "You belong to your father the devil" because they wanted to kill Him. He was basically saying, "I'm right here in front of you/in your midst/among you and you're not even recognizing who I am."

In the same way, Jesus is right here among us. His Word is available and speaking. His Holy Spirit is ministering throughout the earth. But are we responding? Are we listening? Bill O'Reilly took a lot of flack after his 60 Minutes interview with Norah O'Donnell, talking about his historical book, *Killing Jesus*. He said the idea to write the book came to him in the middle of the night, that he believes the Holy Spirit directed him to write it.[101] Whatever your opinion of Bill O'Reilly, it was extremely brave for such a well-known personality to make this claim.

Heaven Is Knocking

"Here I am! I stand at the door and knock..." (Revelation 3:20).

In the 1970's, Bob Dylan wrote a song called, "Knockin' on Heaven's Door." But according to the Bible, Mr. Dylan had it backwards, that heaven is knocking on our door. "Here I am! I stand at the door and knock. If anyone hears my voice and opens the door, I will come in and eat with you. And you will eat with me" (Revelation 3:20 NIRV). The operative words in this verse—the condition upon which God will "eat" with us—are "if" and "and." Meaning that we can hear God's voice, but then choose whether or not to open the door. Whenever I read this passage, it brings to mind something that happened, again, when my daughter was three years old.

Sarah had been coming down with a cold, and I was worried about her. But I had to go to work and leave her with a babysitter. She was my only child, I'd had her late in life, and worried obsessively over her. That whole day I prayed (to a god I didn't yet know) that Sarah would be all right. I couldn't concentrate on my work at all; I was so preoccupied with thoughts about her. When I got home, Sarah ran to my arms and said, "Mommy! When I was running on the beach today I heard you talking in my heart!"

I was stunned. As I felt the sting of tears, I knew, deep in my own heart, that the love and concern I had for my daughter, that those prayers I prayed, had somehow transcended time and space and had connected with her innocent little heart. But I had no idea how that could have happened.

Since becoming a Christian, I've heard people say that they have "felt" others praying for them. I now believe it is because the Spirit of God, the Holy Spirit who Jesus said in John 14:26 would be "the Comforter," communicates those prayers. And the door of Sarah's three-year-old heart was wide open to receive what the Spirit was saying. Jesus said we all need to be like that. "Let the children come to me. Don't stop them! For the Kingdom of Heaven belongs to those who are like these children" (Matthew 19:14 ESV).

Jesus said we need to be like children, like my daughter Sarah was, in order to enter Heaven. He encouraged the children to come to him, rebuking his disciples when they attempted to hold the children back. Jesus clearly loved children. It is frightening to realize that we have destroyed 57 million children through abortion. If He rebuked his disciples for merely discouraging children, what can we expect for murdering them? The fact that we have not yet been rebuked is astounding proof of His grace and mercy, which will not last forever.

Jeremiah 6:16 says, "Stand at the crossroads and look; ask for the ancient paths, ask where the good way is, and walk in it, and you will find rest for your souls. But you said, 'We will not walk in it.'" And like Jeremiah's audience,

I didn't walk in it either, preferring my own path. Until God showed me how real He is, and that He absolutely, positively answers prayers when we seek Him with our whole hearts (Jeremiah 29:13).

 Dream Journal Entry
February 15, 2006

I was on my back, forcibly held down by a dark, heavy weight. It felt like a person was on top of me, as if pinning me to a wrestling mat, my arms and legs splayed. In my mind, I was screaming, "Help!" over and over, but I couldn't talk or breathe. It felt like I was suffocating, dying. Yet in the periphery around me was a gauzy blue light and soft, murmuring voices. I finally woke, sat up, and screamed, "HELP!"

Chapter Fifteen
Providing Deliverance

"...and call upon me in the day of trouble; I will deliver you, and you will honor me" (Psalm 50:15).

Like most alcoholics, I didn't think I had a problem; even though over the years I'd fallen out of bed, down hills, and stranded my daughter several times because I'd blacked out or fallen asleep.

But shortly after I started attending church, my pastor preached a sermon about our bodies being temples for God's Holy Spirit.

"Do you not know that your bodies are temples of the Holy Spirit, who is in you, whom you have received from God? You are not your own; you were bought at a price. Therefore honor God with your bodies" (1 Corinthians 6:19-20).

I began to wonder whether my 90-proof temple was the appropriate place for God to reside. In addition, I was realizing that my mind was foggy when I tried to write and I had become frustrated by repeated failed attempts. So I decided to stop drinking.

For a few weeks, I was fine. But then I'd rationalize that a little wine, compared to an 8-ounce martini or two would be okay. Of course, a little wine turned into a lot of wine, and I was right back to where I started. It wasn't until my husband and I planned a trip to the Caribbean that I got serious and asked God to help me.

Two months before our trip, I stopped drinking again. By this time I had developed a regular prayer life, and my attempt to quit appeared to be working. I went that entire two months without any liquor. But as the days got closer to our vacation, my prayers became desperate. I knew that, being away in that seductive atmosphere, I would be tempted to drink.

So I began to pray, every day, on my knees, from the bottom of my heart, asking God to show me if it was okay for me to have a drink—because I really wanted to be able to. I rationalized that Jesus Himself drank wine, as did many throughout the Bible. And for me, drinking was a fun, social activity. I never drank to drown my sorrows. In fact the few times I've been depressed I never wanted to drink. I was a happy drunk. My problem was that once I started, I didn't stop.

While we were on vacation, we bought a few bottles of wine in anticipation of having company visit. And one night when I was preparing dinner, the balmy Caribbean breeze seemed to whisper, "Go ahead, have a little wine. It won't hurt you." So I had just half a glass. Aside from feeling a little guilt because it was the first drink I'd had in two months, everything seemed fine. Until I had the dream that opens this chapter. However, it wasn't just a dream.

After waking up and shouting, "Help!" I went into the bathroom. When I turned on the light, I heard a voice, clearly and distinctly. It was demonic, straight from the original *The Exorcist* movie. In a sneering, mocking tone, the voice said, *"Praise the Lord!!"*

Even more terrified than when I saw that movie thirty years earlier, I instinctively ran for my Bible. My heart thumping like a sneaker in a dryer, I got on my knees and said the first thing that came to mind, The Lord's Prayer. I said it over and over. Then I remembered, "greater is He in me than he that's in the world" (1 John 4:4 paraphrased). And I said that over and over. And then, like a storm giving way to a rainbow, I knew that what had happened was a very direct answer to my prayers. As this revelation took hold, I felt like a child experiencing a magic trick for the first time. Except that I knew, without a doubt, how real this was.

God showed me, in the way only a Father who truly knows and loves His daughter can, that I cannot drink. That it was suffocating my spirit, pinning me to the mat of my flesh, and keeping me from doing whatever it was that God was calling me to do. (Part of that was writing this book.) God showed me that not only is He real, but that the devil is real, too. And not only did I actually hear that voice, I realized later that I never sleep on my back, nor had I ever woken up on my back before that night.

That experience happened ten years before the completion of this book. Since then, I haven't had a drink, nor have I struggled over having one. Though I admire Alcoholics Anonymous for the millions of people it helps to overcome addictions, I was delivered from mine by the Ultimate Healer, Jesus Christ. And "when the Son sets you free, you are free indeed" (John 8:36). The Bible says, "The angel of the Lord encamps around those who fear him, and he delivers them" (Psalm 34:7). I believe the Lord and His angels were in that blue light and those soft murmuring voices surrounding me in my struggle that night.

Who reading this is not in need of some form of deliverance? It doesn't have to be from alcohol or drugs. It can be deliverance from worry and anxiety. It can be deliverance from feeling like you always need to control things. It can be deliverance from anger or resentment. That deliverance comes, the Bible says, when we "fear" God, which means to be in awe of Him, to hold Him high above ourselves and everything else in our lives.

While it's true that at the time of my deliverance from alcohol I had begun to "fear" God, for most of my life, I hadn't. Yet when I look back through those anointed binoculars, I see the Lord's undeniable hand of grace and mercy through all those years of ignorance and unbelief.

August 9, 2011

I was on a trip overseas with a woman. She said we should have affairs while we were there, that we were so far away, no one would ever know. So we did. My guy was in the service, the Navy, pretty sure. Remember the hat. Think we were kissing? But then he just fell down on the floor. I knew he was dead. I called the police, even though I was afraid they'd think I'd killed him and even though I was incriminating myself in adultery. They were surprisingly nice.

Then I was back home with my Pastor, but also seemed like my husband. He was being very nice to me, like he didn't know. But then he asked me about it, said the overseas police had called. I felt HORRIBLE. Was crying. Saw the tears filling up in my eyes. I apologized profusely. Said we only kissed, nothing else. But I knew the intent mattered, was just as bad. But my Pastor was very calm and not angry, which made me feel worse, even more repentant.

Chapter Sixteen
Demonstrating Mercy

"Or do you show contempt for the riches of his kindness, tolerance and patience, not realizing that God's kindness leads you toward repentance?" (Romans 2:4).

In this dream I felt very much the way I described my daughter feeling when she realized she had stolen that little doll. It's the way I felt when God revealed what abortion is—I wished I'd never done it.

Yet even though I took the lives of two children, I was still allowed to have my beautiful daughter, Sarah. That's what grace and mercy are—getting what we don't deserve and not getting what we do deserve. It's the unbelievable kindness of God, which is what the Bible says leads us to feel bad, to change, or repent. It's the fundamental meaning of one of the most popular verses in the New Testament, John 3:16. "For God so loved the world that he gave his one and only son, so that whoever believes in him shall not perish, but have eternal life." Would you sacrifice your sweet, obedient child for a bunch of disobedient brats? That's what God, in His grace and mercy, did for us.

Jeremiah 31:3 says, "I have loved you with an everlasting love; I have drawn you with loving kindness." I didn't know about or feel this love until I turned 53. But that doesn't mean it wasn't there all those years before. So if you're like I was, be encouraged. Because when I look back at the circumstances surrounding Sarah's birth, I can clearly see that "the arm of the Lord is not too short to save, nor his ear too dull to hear" (Isaiah 59:1).

Although September 16, 1988, was Sarah's scheduled due date, she was born on September 29, two weeks later. Because she was overdue, my doctor had arranged for me to go to the hospital to have my labor induced. On September 28, I was packing my bags when the call came.

"I'm sorry, Mrs. Koop. But it's melanoma." We had been waiting for my husband Jerry's dermatologist to call with his biopsy results. The doctor's words gathered around me like crows.

"Unlike all the others, this biopsy was malignant. That means the cancer has spread, although we don't know how much or where. Jerry needs to make an appointment with a surgeon. I can recommend an excellent one. But I'm afraid this isn't good news. Only about ten percent of melanoma patients survive."

Sarah took a tumble in my womb as if she'd heard; as if the reality of her life belied the prospect of her father's death. Attempts to respond to the doctor skidded past my mouth until he filled the awkward silence. "I'm sorry, Mrs. Koop. I wish I had better news."

I finally managed, "Yeah, me too," then hung up the phone, my hand trembling.

Everything I'd ever feared crept up my legs, grabbed my heart, and squeezed. After scores of nonmalignant and premalignant lesions, Jerry's years as a lifeguard had caught up to him.

The phone rang again, this time it was Jerry. He was calling from his office, unaware that I had just spoken to the doctor. He repeated those two words that would impact our lives forever. "It's melanoma."

That evening we took a taxi to the hospital. We held hands in silence, individually processing the nightmare that had just unpacked its terrible valise. Unlike today, in 1988 there were no treatment options. But what I didn't know then was "With man this is impossible, but with God all things are possible" (Matthew 19:26).

Because the hospital was undergoing construction, the only place they had room for me was in the obstetrics ward. I had to share a room with a woman who was in active labor, just a thin curtain separating us. She moaned and screamed all night, an ever-present reminder of what I was about to experience.

In the morning I was given a drug to induce labor, and then hooked up to a fetal monitor. I had been determined to go through "natural childbirth," because I thought it would be safer for the baby if I could avoid epidural anesthesia. So Jerry and I had been to Lamaze classes, which taught breathing and other techniques to help reduce the pain.

But the classroom is no match for real life. When the contractions kicked in, I screamed for the anesthesiologist. Almost immediately after getting the epidural, I was numb from the waist down. But nothing could be done for the pain in my heart. From the waist up, everything hurt.

After I'd been in labor for a few hours, the fetal monitor started beeping. My doctor came in, took one look at the screen and said, "Let's go have this baby!" She instructed Jerry to put on the surgical garb left for him and rushed me into the operating room.

My umbilical cord had become wrapped around Sarah's neck. As Jerry watched the doctor quickly and deftly twist Sarah's little body, freeing her to take her first breath, he wondered if he'd see her first step.

"She's beautiful!" Though my husband is a man of few words, inside his tearful cry was a lifetime of unspoken joys, regrets, and longings. Just seconds later, Sarah's throaty wail pierced my heart. When I was pregnant with Sarah, a friend who recently had a baby said, "You think you love Jerry? Just wait."

When Sarah was placed on my chest and I lifted myself to look at her scrunched up little face, I began to shake. The tremors were uncontrollable. It was if a volcano had erupted inside of me, releasing a marrow-deep emotional avalanche.

The room was cold, as was the steel table, but that's not why I was trembling. I had been on other cold steel tables in other cold rooms. But this time I had given life, not taken it. And I know now that what was exploding within me at that moment was the unconditional love of God Himself.

"I am the way, the truth and the life" (John 14:6). Jesus is life, the creator and author of life. And I had just taken part in that unfathomable miracle. What is amazing to me now is that I don't recall thinking about my unborn children at that moment. I suppose because it was a time, much like today, when laws and semantics overrode morality. My abortions had been legal and I hadn't thought of the "fetuses" as babies.

Shortly after we brought Sarah home, we saw the surgeon recommended by Jerry's dermatologist. The x-rays showed a large tumor around Jerry's left sternomastoid muscle, which affects the movement of the neck. He said that it also looked like the tumor had become wrapped around nerves on the left side of Jerry's face. He said that the muscle would most likely have to be removed, and that the procedure would be very intricate because of the facial muscles. Depending on how it went, he said there was a possibility Jerry could be paralyzed on that side of his face.

The operation took seven hours. The doctor finally came in to the waiting room, moving what looked like telescopic glasses to the top of his head. He said the surgery had gone well. He did have to remove the neck muscle, but felt that he had gotten the entire tumor. He also removed some lymph nodes to test for the spread of the cancer, and we'd know the results in a week. The facial nerves hadn't been compromised. It was very good news.

The meaning of the word "Gospel" is "good news"—the good news that Jesus died for us, for every bad thing we ever did or will do, that He was buried and brought back to life. So that "whoever believes in him shall not perish but have eternal life" (John 3:16). It is a message about life and death, which is the message at the very heart of this book. And there has never been a time since those seven days when life and death have been more palpable. While Sarah was a testament to the miracle of life, Jerry's bandages and drainage tubes were reminders of its brevity.

I remember the day we got Jerry's pathology results. I was sitting in our backyard watching the sun go down, as I'd done many times before. It was the same yard, the same chair, the same sun. But there was no cancer, and that changed everything. Overwhelming gratitude gripped my heart as a sense of the miraculous spilled from my eyes. That evening as I watched the sun sink into the fiery horizon, I was that little girl again, sitting in the cavernous church sanctuary, awed by the presence of God.

But there was still another hurdle to face. Even though there was no cancer detected in the lymph nodes they tested, there was no guarantee the cancer hadn't or wouldn't eventually spread elsewhere. And treatment was virtually nonexistent at that time.

We consulted with several cancer specialists, but none could give us any hope other than clinical trials with mediocre results. But then the same friend who warned me about the explosive love I'd feel for Sarah (who had sadly lost her husband to cancer), recommended a research organization. Through it, we found a one-of-a-kind doctor, Nicholas Gonzalez, whom God used to save Jerry's life.

The treatment was considered non-standard or "alternative." But it had amazingly good, proven results for treating not only the type of melanoma Jerry had, but also the worst cases of pancreatic cancer, which are most often fatal. Dr. Gonzalez's detailed metabolic workup for Jerry provided an individualized nutritional program that was accompanied by coffee enemas, liver and gall bladder cleanses, plus scores of daily supplements and pancreatic enzymes. The criteria were rigorous and completely dependent on patient initiative. In order to fully comply, Jerry had to take a disability leave and I went back to work.

Looking back on those years, particularly that time 27 years ago, so much of God's Word has come to pass. Romans 8:28 says, "And we know that in all things God works for the good of those who love him, who have been called according to his purpose." When I went back to work, Jerry was home with Sarah. He was able to bond with her, in those crucial formative years, in a way he wouldn't have otherwise been able to.

And Ephesians 3:20 says that God "is able to do immeasurably more than all we ask or imagine." During the course of Jerry's disability leave, his insurance company offered him a payout that enabled us to purchase and renovate a home that would otherwise have been just a dream.

But above everything else, after being given a death sentence almost three decades ago, Jerry is alive and well today. Again, "With man this is impossible, but with God all things are possible" (Matthew 19:26).

The Word of God is Truth. When we turn to God, when we, as Jeremiah says, seek Him with our whole hearts (29:13), we will find Him. And when we do, He transforms our minds and hearts with that eternal sunrise – hope. And, as Psalm 23:6 says, His grace and mercy will follow us all the days of our lives.

As I've repeatedly said, I was ignorant about God, about the Bible for most of my life. I believe "I was shown mercy because I acted in ignorance and unbelief ..." (1 Timothy 1:13). But for those of you who aren't ignorant about God, and for those of you who have gotten a basic understanding of who God is after reading this book, please do not reject Him. Because as loving and merciful and graceful as God is, He is also righteous, holy, and just. Like He said before the flood, "My Spirit will not contend with man forever" (Genesis 6:3). And the conditions under which God said that are eerily similar to the conditions today.

"Now the earth was corrupt in God's sight and was full of violence. God saw how corrupt the earth had become, for all the people on earth had corrupted their ways. So God said to Noah, "I am going to put an end to

all people, for the earth is filled with violence because of them. I am surely going to destroy both them and the earth" (Genesis 6:11-13).

God instructed Noah, who "was a righteous man... and he walked with God" (Genesis 6:9), to build an ark to save himself, his family and all living creatures. After it rained for forty days and forty nights, and the flood destroyed everything that God said it would, He made a covenant, or an agreement with Noah.

"I have set my rainbow in the clouds, and it will be the sign of the covenant between me and the earth...Never again will the waters become a flood to destroy all life" (Genesis 9:13 15).

God promised Noah that He would never again destroy the earth through water.

But He did not promise that He would never destroy the earth again.

January 28, 2013

I was having dinner in a restaurant with my husband. But I was in my pajamas, feeling uncomfortable about that. I got up to go to the bathroom. On my way I saw a woman very upset, crying, with people around her also very upset. When I reentered the restaurant it was empty. I went outside and found my husband. He, too, was very upset. I asked what was wrong. He said that there was a news report that something terrible was going to happen that had to do with the sky, and the world was going to be destroyed. I looked up at the sky and saw the moon, but it felt like fire—like an asteroid or something was going to hit, and there was going to be a huge fire, starting on the west coast coming east. I knew it was from God and told that to my husband. And that if we prayed to Him, maybe He could stop it. I said, "Maybe this is what 2 Chronicles 7:14 means." And I spoke the Scripture: "If my people, who are called by my name, will humble themselves and pray and seek my face and turn from their wicked ways, then will I hear from heaven and will forgive their sin and will heal their land." I felt an urgency to complete this book, like there might not be enough time, that people need to read it. Then I was in front of several rows of stacked firewood. I began rolling them from back to front, making single layers of logs. Again, I knew that the fire was going to come from the left/west and burn the logs.

Chapter Seventeen
Proclaiming Judgment

"If we deliberately keep on sinning after we have received the knowledge of the truth, no sacrifice for sins is left, but only a fearful expectation of judgment and of raging fire that will consume the enemies of God" (Hebrews 10:26-27).

The dream on the facing page was one of the most disturbing I've ever had. As I was recording it the next morning, I asked the Lord to help me understand it.

As I often do, I stuck my finger into the pages, opened my Bible and started reading. I had opened to Isaiah 66. The chapter is titled, "Judgment and Hope." Verses 15 and 16 say, "See, the LORD is coming with fire...he will bring down his anger with fury, and his rebuke with flames of fire. For with fire and with his sword, the LORD will execute judgment upon all men, and many will be those slain by the LORD."

Matthew 24 and Mark 13 talk about signs of the end of the age, and the return of Jesus Christ. Matthew compares it to the time of Noah, when no one expected or believed the flood would happen. "People were eating and drinking, marrying and giving in marriage" (Matt. 24:38b). In the dream, I was having dinner. And Mark warns us to watch. "If he comes suddenly, do not let him find you sleeping" (Mark 13:36). In the dream, I was in my pajamas. Both Gospels refer to stars falling from the sky and the heavens

187

being shaken: "the sun will be darkened, and the moon will not give its light; the stars will fall from the sky, and the heavenly bodies will be shaken" (Matthew 24:29, Mark 13:24-25).

On February 15, 2013, two weeks after I had this dream, a meteorite unexpectedly hit Russia. It was all over the news, with 1,000 people injured.[102] That same day, an asteroid passed within 17,000 miles of the earth—the closest an asteroid has ever gotten to our planet.[103] The next day, there was a sighting of an asteroid in the night sky over San Francisco Bay.[104] Two days later, there was a sighting of a "fireball" in the Florida sky.[105]

I know some will scoff at this. But I believe with all my heart that this dream, like all the others I've cited in this book, is part of a message that needs to be heard. It is a warning, a clarion call for national repentance. "... sound the alarm on my holy hill...for the day of the LORD is coming" (Joel 2:1). It is an age-old call that has echoed throughout the centuries. The fact that God has not yet acted is a testament to His loving mercy over our lives. It is where we find hope, along with the judgment. But He will act, the Bible is clear on that:

"With the Lord, a day is like a thousand years and a thousand years are like a day. The Lord is not slow in keeping his promise, as some understand slowness. He is patient with you, not wanting anyone to perish, but everyone to come to repentance. But the day of the Lord will come like a thief.

*The heavens will disappear with a roar; the elements will be
destroyed by fire, and the earth and everything in it will be
laid bare"* (2 Peter 3:8-10).

President Abraham Lincoln sounded this same clarion
call 150 years ago in his Proclamation for a National Day
of Humiliation, Fasting, and Prayer, issued in the midst of
the American Civil War (emphasis mine):

> We have been the recipients of the choicest
> bounties of Heaven. We have been preserved,
> these many years, in peace and prosperity.
> We have grown in numbers, wealth, and
> power as no other nation has ever grown.
> **But we have forgotten God.** We have
> forgotten the gracious hand which preserved
> us in peace, and multiplied and enriched and
> strengthened us; and have vainly imagined,
> in the deceitfulness of our hearts, that all
> these blessings were produced by some
> superior wisdom and virtue of our own.
> **Intoxicated with unbroken success,
> we have become too self-sufficient to
> feel the necessity of redeeming and
> preserving grace, too proud to pray
> to the God that made us! It behooves
> us, then, to humble ourselves before
> the offended Power, to confess our
> national sins, and to pray for clemency
> and forgiveness.**[106]

President Lincoln could have been quoting from
Deuteronomy:

*"Be careful that you **do not forget the LORD your God,**
failing to observe his commands...Otherwise, when you*

189

eat and are satisfied, when you build fine houses and settle down...and all you have is multiplied, then your heart will become proud and **you will forget the LORD your God**... *You may say to yourself,* **'My power and the strength of my hands have produced this wealth for me.'**...**If you ever forget the LORD** *your God and follow other gods and worship and bow down to them, I testify to you today that* **you surely will be destroyed***"* (8:11-14, 17, 19).

But we have forgotten the Lord our God, haven't we? Because the mindset of today says, "When we eat and are satisfied, when we build fine houses and settle down, when all we have is multiplied, our hearts become proud. Our power and the strength of our hands have produced this wealth for us. We follow other gods and worship and bow down to them. We will never be destroyed."

The Valley of Decision

"Multitudes, multitudes in the valley of decision: for the day of the LORD is near in the valley of decision" (Joel 3:14).

This verse speaks not about our decision, but of the Lord's, regarding those who have rejected Him. It speaks of the judgment of God on those who have chosen their own way. Yet in the previous chapter, Joel says, "And everyone who calls on the name of the LORD will be saved" (2:32). That is what we, as individuals and as a nation, must do if we don't want to wind up in the Valley of Decision. Because, as we said earlier, "It is a dreadful thing to fall into the hands of the living God" (Hebrews 10:31).

The Bible is a living book. It is alive and breathing, a supernatural compilation of words and wisdom that transcend time. Its truths apply just as much today as they did in Jeremiah's day. "Look! I am preparing a disaster for you and devising a plan against you. So turn from your evil ways, each one of you, and reform your ways and your actions. But they will reply, 'It's no use. We will continue with our own plans; each of us will follow the stubbornness of his evil heart'" (Jeremiah 18:11b -12). And in the New Testament, Jesus, who is The Truth, confirms this. "Because of the increase of wickedness, the love of most will grow cold, but he who stands firm to the end will be saved. And this gospel of the kingdom will be preached in the whole world as a testimony to all nations, and then the end will come" (Matthew 24:12-14).

I believe with all my heart that God is having me write this book because the end is nearer than we think. Today, more than any time in history, technology is enabling the "gospel of the kingdom" to "be preached in the whole world as a testimony to all nations." What God said over two thousand years ago, He is saying today:

"This commandment that I'm commanding you today isn't too much for you, it's not out of your reach. It's not on a high mountain—you don't have to get mountaineers to climb the peak and bring it down to your level and explain it before you can live it. And it's not across the ocean—you don't have to send sailors out to get it, bring it back, and then explain it before you can live it. No. The

word is right here and now—as near as the tongue in your mouth, as near as the heart in your chest. Just do it!" (Deuteronomy 30:11-14 MSG).

So we need to make some crucial decisions right now.

Are we going to continue to follow the stubbornness of our hearts, or are we going to listen to the wisdom of God?

Are we going to continue to profess morality, and then twist it to condone our behavior?

Are we going to continue to label drugs with warnings about babies in the womb, and then tear those same babies from the womb?

Are we going to continue refusing to step on spiders or to fell trees, while promoting late-term abortions?

Are we going to continue worshipping at the altar of our own desires and turning our backs on the One who desires us?

Or are we going to respond to God's final warnings, to His great mercy? Because if we don't, this is what the Sovereign Lord says:

"I will punish you as your deeds deserve, declares the LORD. I will kindle a fire in your forests that will consume everything around you" (Jeremiah 21:14).

"As the weeds are pulled up and burned in the fire, so it will be at the end of the age. The Son of Man will send out his angels, and they will weed out of his kingdom everything that causes sin and all who do evil. They will throw them into the blazing furnace, where there will be weeping and gnashing of teeth" (Matthew 13: 40-42).

"Do you think that these Galileans were worse sinners than all the other Galileans because they suffered this way? I tell you, no! But unless you repent, you too will all perish" (Luke 13:2-3).

"Surely the day is coming; it will burn like a furnace. All the arrogant and every evildoer will be stubble, and the day that is coming will set them on fire," says the LORD Almighty. "Not a root or a branch will be left to them" (Malachi 4:1).

Considering the state of our nation and world today, these scenarios are far from unrealistic.

It has been ten years since my conversion and since I had the dream of the brick wall with "Jeremiah 15" etched into it. The Biblical symbolism of the number ten is to measure, for the purpose of accepting or rejecting that which is measured. Over these years, God was placing His message upon my heart. I had to measure, or choose, whether to accept or reject His direction to "write down the revelation and make it plain" (Habakkuk 2:2). Now that I have, you also must "measure" its message.

I pray with all my heart that you will accept the truth as it has been laid out here, and "choose life so that you and your children will live..." (Deuteronomy 30:19).

Epilogue: 2015

On my desk is a three-by-five wrinkled and faded black and white picture of me at about seven or eight, standing in front of my childhood home. I have a schoolbag in one hand, a bouquet of flowers picked from the garden in the other. I'm dressed neatly in a skirt and blouse, white anklets and Mary Jane shoes. My hair is pulled back into a ponytail and I'm smiling, looking genuinely happy and excited. My mother wrote on the back, "Off to school with flowers for teacher."

Today I connect more with that little girl, excited about pleasing her teacher, than I do with the confused 24-year-old woman whose skirt and blouse strained at their seams in a taxi forty years ago. And I give thanks to God for that 40-year journey. Because it has returned me to the childlike excitement of wanting to please, but wanting to please the right Teacher in the right way.

The young woman in that taxi wanted to please everyone by doing whatever they wanted her to, including giving herself away time after time. But that desire was misdirected, fueled by lies, ignorance, and insecurity. The desire I have now is fueled by Truth, and knowing the security of a love that was nailed to a tree for me.

Two weeks before sending this manuscript off to my publisher, I found a mug on my daughter's desk. On it was a picture of her hugging me from behind, her arms latched around my neck, her cheek pressed against my back with a smile that clearly says, "I love my mom." I realized the picture was from a bridal shower we'd been to several months earlier. Because my birthday was coming up, I assumed she'd had the mug made especially for me as a surprise, knowing how much I love my morning coffee. I can't tell you how touched I was that she would have been so thoughtful as to have gone to the trouble to give me such a special, personalized gift.

I didn't want to spoil her surprise, figuring she left it there by mistake. So I didn't say anything until a few days later, when we were sitting on her bed talking. The mug was still right there, out in the open. So I asked her about it. She told me that her friend's aunt had it made as a memento of the shower and sent it to her. Of course I was a bit deflated, but we had a big laugh after I shared with her what I'd thought.

And then I reflected on how touched I was when I imagined that Sarah had gone so out of her way to show me how much she loved me. But isn't that what Christ did for us? He didn't just emblazon an image on a cup, He shed His blood on a cross. He gave His life for ours. And it is in that amazing transaction, in that divine exchange, where meaning and purpose are found.

As I was completing this manuscript, we received the devastating news that Dr. Nicholas Gonzalez, the man God led us to, the man He used to save Jerry's life, had unexpectedly passed away at the young age of 67. Dr. Gonzalez was hailed by many, especially his patients, as a hero and a pioneer in the fight against cancer. Several of his formerly terminal patients, including Jerry, reflected on the unspeakably sad irony that they continue to enjoy the life he, in many ways, gave them.

What I did not know about Nick Gonzalez, but found out through the comments of his patients, was that he was a man of faith in Jesus Christ. And it is evident in something he wrote that was included in a eulogy posted by Kelly Brogan, MD. It sounds so much like Matthew 24, when Jesus speaks about the end of the age. He wrote it less than a month before he died.

"We are in times of trouble to be followed by the light of peace, the calm of hope realized, the transcendence of truth. Not now, not yet, but soon. We are in the Suntaleia, the Greek term for the Consummation of the Ages, a time of confusion, political strife, hatred of truth, governmental oppression and the rise toward one world dictatorship. Then comes the destruction of truth's enemies, the restoration of the earth and recognition for those that gallantly stood firm for the truth and its always-righteous application. So do not despair, it isn't necessary to do so, the plan is falling into place, these times are but the birth pangs of the glorious world that will follow." *

And that glorious world is what Jesus died to give us. What we need to do, to be partakers of that world, is to confess with our mouths that Jesus is Lord and believe in our hearts that God raised him from the dead (Romans 10:9). Once I did that, the question posed at the beginning of this book—why do we innately know right from wrong, yet continue to do wrong?—was answered. It's because we don't know the Truth. It's because we're relying on ourselves. It's because we don't understand our own hearts, and therefore don't realize we need a Savior. The Message version of the Bible puts it this way, "The heart is hopelessly dark and deceitful, a puzzle that no one can figure out. But I, God, search the heart and examine the mind. I get to the heart of the human. I get to the root of things. I treat them as they really are, not as they pretend to be" (Jeremiah 17:9-10).

I'm so thankful God brought me to that realization. So now I can say to you, with childlike faith, "Come, see a man who knew all about the things I did, who knows me inside and out" (John 4:29, MSG).

* For more information on the treatment protocol my husband received, please visit The Nicholas Gonzalez Foundation at www.dr-gonzalez.com.

"It is your message I have given them, not my own" (Jeremiah 17:16 NLT).

Amen.

If Not For You

To be my age and try to find
the courage to leave fear behind
and do what I'm compelled to do,
would be impossible, Lord, if not for You.

Before You came into my heart,
I used my talents in fits and starts—
a poem here, a story there,
but all the while unaware

That You would live inside of me
and scrub me clean till I could see
that the only thing I'd want to do
is use my gifts to honor You.

Now, beyond anything I could have imagined,
or by my hand have naturally fashioned,
You've placed a fire inside my bones.
I feel like Jeremiah, who wept and moaned

Over the message he was born to bring
to a people who would suffer the sting
of turning their backs on the one true God
Who did not, and will not, spare the rod.

Jeremiah said, "I'm too young." I say, "I'm too old."
And besides that, Lord, I've never been bold.
So it's Your words, not mine, that must fill the pages,
convict the hearts of people of all ages

To humble themselves and seek Your face,
to repent and receive Your grace.
And in their turning to understand
that only You can heal our land.

This is the message to which I'm bound:
we've become lost, but can be found.
And I know, Lord, that You'll see this through.
Because I could not do it, if not for You.

ENDNOTES

1. Rick Warren, *The Purpose Driven Life,* Zondervan, 2002, pg. 17.

2. Charles Stanley, *The Blessings of Brokenness,* Zondervan, 1997, pp. 71, 60-61.

3. Brooke Ligertwood, "Hosanna" © 2006 Hillsong Music Publishing, Administered by EMI Christian Music, which is now Capital Christian Music Group, (CMG). All rights reserved.

4. Billy James Foote, songwriter, "You Are My King (Amazing Love)," Copyright © 1999 worshiptogether. com Songs (ASCAP) (adm. at CapitolCMGPublishing. com) All rights reserved. Used by permission.(License purchased.)

5. David McCasland, "The Lure of the Message," *Our Daily Bread* magazine, Sept. 18, 2012.

6. Oswald Chambers (author), James Reimann (Editor), Sept. 30, "The Assigning of the Call," *My Utmost for His Highest,* Discovery House, Revised edition, 1992.

7. Mark Hall, songwriter, "While You Were Sleeping," Copyright © 2005 My Refuge Music (BMI) (adm. at CapitolCMGPublishing.com) / Be Essential Songs (BMI). All rights reserved. Used by permission. (License purchased.)

8. Paul Greenberg quoted by William Brennan, Ph.D in "Challenging the Language of the Culture of Death" on lifeissues.net, accessed 3/22/16, http://www.lifeissues. net/writers/air/air_vol8no2_1995.html#a2

9. Cornell University Law School, Legal Information Institute, Roe vs. Wade, Section IXA. Accessed 11/30/15, http://www.law.cornell.edu/supct/html/ historics/USSC_CR_0410_0113_ZO.html,

10. Linda Hinkle, "When Does an Unborn Baby Have a Heartbeat?" LiveStrong.com, 8/16/13, accessed 11/30/15, http://www.livestrong.com/article/242600-when-does-an-unborn-baby-have-a-heartbeat/

11. Steven Ertelt, "Expert Tells Congress Unborn Babies Can Feel Pain Starting At 8 Weeks," LifeNews.com, 5/23/13, accessed 11/30/15, http://www.lifenews.com/2013/05/23/expert-tells-congress-unborn-babies-can-feel-pain-starting-at-8-weeks/

12. "The First Trimester: Your Baby's Growth and Development in Early Pregnancy," WebMD.com, accessed 11/30/15, http://www.webmd.com/baby/1to3-months

13. "Discussing the Issue of Abortion," UK Essays, 3/23/15, accessed 1/16/16, http://www.ukessays.com/essays/philosophy/discussing-the-issue-of-abortion-philosophy-essay.php

14. Michelle Obama, American Grown: *The Story of the White House Kitchen Garden and Gardens Across America*, Crown Publishers, New York City, 2012, p. 23.

15. Wm. Robert Johnston, "Reasons Given for Having Abortions in the United States," 8/26/12, accessed 11/30/15, http://www.johnstonsarchive.net/policy/abortion/abreasons.html#9

16. "The Two-Minus-One Pregnancy," New York Times Magazine, 8/10/11, accessed 11/30/15, http://www.nytimes.com/2011/08/14/magazine/the-two-minus-one-pregnancy.html?pagewanted=all

17. Ibid.

18. Cornell University Law School, Legal Information Institute, Roe vs. Wade, Section VIII, accessed 1/16/16, http://www.law.cornell.edu/supct/html/historics/USSC_CR_0410_0113_ZO.html

19. Wikipedia, "Roe vs. Wade," accessed 11/30/15, http://en.wikipedia.org/wiki/Roe_v._Wade#Supreme_Court_decision,

20. Andrew P. Napolitano, "A Few Words About Abortion," Lew Rockwell.com, 1/28/12, accessed 12/21/15, https://www.lewrockwell.com/2012/01/andrew-p-napolitano/when-the-government-declares-you-a-nonperson/

21. Bill Combs, "Did Saul Change His Name to Paul?" Detroit Baptist Theological Seminary, 6/10/12, accessed 1/8/16, http://dbts.edu/blog/did-saul-change-his-name-to-paul/

22. "An Ex-Abortionist speaks" a review of "Confessions of An Ex-Abortionist" in *The Hand of God: A Journey from Death to Life by the Abortion Doctor Who Changed His Mind.* Dr. Bernard Nathanson, Regenery Publishing, 1997, Catholic News Agency.com, http://m.catholicnewsagency.com/resource.php?n=402 Accessed 1/8/16

23. Ibid.

24. Ross Douthat, "The Media's Abortion Blinders," *New York Times Sunday Review,* Op Ed, 2/4/12, accessed 1/16/16, http://www.nytimes.com/2012/02/05/opinion/sunday/douthat-the-medias-blinders-on-abortion.html?_r=0

25. Dr. Bernard Nathanson, *The Hand of God: A Journey from Death to Life by the Abortion Doctor Who Changed His Mind.* Regenery Publishing, 1997, p. 48.

26. Ibid. p. 50.

27. Ibid. pp. 53-54.

28. Steven Ertelt, "57,762,169 Abortions in America Since Roe vs. Wade in 1973," LifeNews.com, 1/21/15, accessed 12/21/15, http://www.lifenews.com/2015/01/21/57762169-abortions-in-america-since-roe-vs-wade-in-1973/

29. Carol Tobias, "Endless Love," National Right to Life, 1/13/13, accessed 11/30/15, http://www.nrlc.org/news/13/winter13news/presidentcolumnpage3/

30. *The Apology of Tertullian*, Chapter IX, p. 32, accessed 11/30/15, http://www.tertullian.org/articles/reeve_apology.htm

31. Bernard Nathanson, *The Hand of God*, Life Cycle Books, Ltd., 1996, p. 127.

32. "Barack Obama Inaugural Address 2013," The Telegraph, accessed 11/30/15, http://www.telegraph.co.uk/news/worldnews/barackobama/9816372/Barack-Obama-Inaugural-Address-2013-full-text.html

33. Ibid.

34. Tom Ascol, "Mr. President, Please Think Deeply About The Sandy Hook Massacre," accessed 1/15/16, http://tomascol.com/mr-president-please-think-deeply-about-the-sandy-hook-massacre/

35. Ravi Zacharias, "Tragedy At Newtown," RZIM News, 12-20-12, accessed 1/16/16, http://us5.campaign-archive2.m/?u=45b75085e6ab57e339ea89d67&id=43e1a26 8bb&e=db221c7bff

36. Matthew S. Black, "Children: Things We Throw Away? Parallels between Modern Abortion and Ancient Child Sacrifice," sermon at Living Hope Bible Church, 1/18/98, accessed 1/8/16, https://sermons.logos. com/submissions/107508-2009-01-18AM-Ancient-Child-Sacrifice-vs-Modern-Abortion-Psalm106-32-48#content=/submissions/107508

37. P.G. Mosca, "Child Sacrifice in Caananite and Israelite Religion," Ph.D. dissertation, Harvard University, 1975, op. cit., pp. 273-274.

38. Bill O'Reilly, "What the Babies Would Say," BillOreilly. com, 1/31/13, accessed 11/30/15 http://www.billoreilly. com/column?pid=39721

39. "Harmartia," Wikipedia.com, accessed 11/30/15, http://en.wikipedia.org/wiki/Hamartia

40. Ariela Pelaia (Judaism Expert), "Do Jews Believe in Sin? The Concept of Sin in Judaism," Judiasm.About. com, accessed 11/30/15 http://judaism.about.com/od/judaismbasics/a/Do-Jews-Believe-In-Sin.htm

41. "Sarx," BibleStudyTools.com, accessed 11/30/15, http://www.biblestudytools.com/lexicons/greek/nas/sarx.html

42. "Basar," BibleStudyTools.com, accessed11/30/15, http://www.biblestudytools.com/lexicons/hebrew/nas/basar-2.html

43. "Pride," Studylight.org, accessed 1/16/16, http://www.studylight.org/dic/bed/view.cgi?number=T567

44. "Alazoneia," BibleStudyTools.com, accessed 11/30/15, http://www.biblestudytools.com/lexicons/greek/nas/alazoneia.html

45. "Avah," BibleStudyTools.com, accessed 12/1/15, http://www.biblestudytools.com/lexicons/hebrew/kjv/avah.html

46. "Epithymia," BlueLetterBible.org, accessed 12/1/15, http://www.blueletterbible.org/lang/lexicon/lexicon.cfm?Strongs=G1939

47. "Anavah," Studylight.org, accessed 12/1/15, http://classic.studylight.org/lex/heb/view.cgi?number=6038

48. "Humility," Blogs.blueletterbible.org, accessed 12/1/15, http://blogs.blueletterbible.org/blb/2011/11/14/humility/

49. "Repentance," Wikipedia, accessed 12/1/15, http://en.wikipedia.org/wiki/Repentance

50. "Redemption," Wikipedia, accessed 12/1/15, http://en.wikipedia.org/wiki/Redemption_(theology)

51. "Peduwth," BlueLetterBible.org, accessed 12/1/15, http://www.blueletterbible.org/lang/lexicon/lexicon.cfm?strongs=H6304

52. "Apolytrosis," BlueLetterBible.org, accessed 12/1/15, http://www.blueletterbible.org/lang/lexicon/lexicon.cfm?strongs=G629&t=NASB

53. "In God We Trust," Rationalwiki.org, accessed 1/16/16, http://rationalwiki.org/wiki/In_God_We_Trust

54. "Supreme Court 'Judicial Decisions!' On becoming a despotic branch" Earstohear.net, accessed 1/16/16, http://earstohear.net/Separation/supreme_court.html

55. Claire Shipman, "Teens: Oral Sex and Casual Prostitution No Biggie," ABCnews.com, 5/28/09, accessed 1/16/16, http://abcnews.go.com/GMA/Parenting/story?id=7693121&page=1#.T0uOh818ono

56. Cassy Fiano, "'A life worth sacrificing': Salon blogger admits abortion ends life," LiveActionNews.org, 1/24/2013, accessed 5/17/16, http://liveactionnews.org/a-life-worth-sacrificing-salon-blogger-admits-abortion-ends-life/

57. "We Can't Stop," Wikipedia, accessed 12/1/15, http://en.wikipedia.org/wiki/We_Can't_Stop

58. Ibid.

59. Christa Banister, "Depravity Knows No Bounds in The Wolf of Wall Street," Crosswalk.com, 12/25/13, accessed 1/8/16, http://www.crosswalk.com/culture/movies/the-wolf-of-wall-street-movie-review.html?p=2

60. Ibid.

61. Alissa Wilkinson, "The Wolf of Wall Street," ChristianityToday.com, 12/26/13, accessed 12/1/15, http://www.christianitytoday.com/ct/2013/december-web-only/wolf-of-wall-street.html?start=1

62. Ruben V. Nepales, "How Scorsese Avoided NC-17 Rating for Wolf of Wall Street," Inquirer.net, 12/14/13, accessed 12/1/15, http://entertainment.inquirer.net/125175/how-scorsese-avoided-nc-17-rating-for-wolf-of-wall-street

63. Todd Starnes, "School Surveys 7th Graders on Oral Sex," FoxNews.com, 6/15/11, accessed 12/1/15, http://www.foxnews.com/us/2011/06/15/school-surveys-7th-graders-on-oral-sex/

64. Jonathan Allen, "Morning-after pills available to N.Y. high school students," ChicagoTribune.com, 9/24/12, accessed 1/8/16   http://www.chicagotribune.com/lifestyles/health/sns-rt-us-schools-birthcontrol-newyorkbre88n0yk-20120924-story.html

65. Ann Pleshette Murphy and Jennifer Allen, "Teen Sex Slave Trade Hits Home," ABCNews.go.com, 1/30/07, accessed 12/1/15, http://abcnews.go.com/GMA/AmericanFamily/story?id=2834852&page=1#.T0uQoc18ono

66. Cole Kazdin and Imaeyen Ibanga, "The Truth About Teens Sexting," ABCnews.go.com, 4/15/09, accessed 1/16/16, http://abcnews.go.com/GMA/Parenting/truth-teens-sexting/story?id=7337547

67. "IUDs, Implants Urged for Teen Girls' Birth Control," FoxNews.com, 9/21/12, accessed 12/1/15, http://www.foxnews.com/health/2012/09/21/iuds-implants-urged-for-teen-girls-birth-control/?test=latestnews#ixzz277RfGp3E

68. President Obama, "Gay Marriage: Gay Couples 'Should Be Able to Get Married,'" ABC NEWS nterview with Robin Roberts, May 2012, accessed 1/18/16, https://www.youtube.com/watch?v=kQGMTPab9GQ

69. "Obama administration will no longer defend DOMA," CBSnews.com, 2/24/11, accessed 1/15/16, http://www.cbsnews.com/news/obama-administration-will-no-longer-defend-doma/,

70. "President Barack Obama's shifting stance on gay marriage," Politifact.com, 5/11/12, accessed 1/15/16, http://www.politifact.com/truth-o-meter/statements/2012/may/11/barack-obama/president-barack-obamas-shift-gay-marriage/

71. "California Proposition 8," Wikipedia, accessed 12/1/15, http://en.wikipedia.org/wiki/California_Proposition_8

72. CNN.com "Supreme Court Rules in Favor of Same-Sex Marriage Nationwide," 6/27/15, accessed 5/17/16 http://www.cnn.com/2015/06/26/politics/supreme-court-same-sex-marriage-ruling/

73. Luke Nix, "Ravi Zacharias on Race and Homosexuality," *Faithful Thinkers* blog, 5/7/12, accessed 1/15/16, http://lukenixblog.blogspot.com/2012/05/ravi-zacharias-on-race-and.html

74. Cheryl K. Chumley, "Florida judge rules birth certificate will list all 3 gay parents," WashingtonTimes.com, 2/8/13, accessed 12/1/15, http://www.washingtontimes.com/news/2013/feb/8/florida-judge-rules-birth-certificate-will-list-al/

75. Russell Goldman and Katie Tompson, "'Pregnant Man' Gives Birth to Girl," ABCnews.go.com, 7/3/08, accessed 12/1/15, http://abcnews.go.com/Health/story?id=5302756&page=1

76. Donald DeMarco, "What Science Tells Us About Same-Sex Unions," Theinterim.com, 4/6/04. Used by written permission. Accessed 1/15/16, http://www.theinterim.com/issues/marriage-family/what-science-tells-us-about-same-sex-unions/

77. John McKellar, "Homosexuals Against Pride Extremism," Catholic-legate.com, 3/15/08, accessed 6/2/16, http://www.catholic-legate.com/homosexual-against-pride-extremism/

78. John McKellar, "The Irony of Same Sex Marriage," Truegate.org, 12/02, accessed 6/2/16, http://www.truegate.org/news/view_short_news.php?id=4278

79. "Obama administration directs schools to accommodate transgender students," WashingtonPost.com, 5/13/16, accessed 6/2/16, https://www.washingtonpost.com/politics/obama-administration-to-instruct-schools-to-accommodate-transgender-students/2016/05/12/0ed1c50e-18ab-11e6-aa55-670cabef46e0_story.html

80. Kathleen Gilbert, "School Must Allow 'Transgender' 6th Grader to Use Girls' Bathroom: Maine Human Rights Panel," Lifesitenews.com, 9/28/10, accessed 1/15/16, http://www.lifesitenews.com/news/school-must-allow-transgender-6th-grader-to-use-girls-bathroom-maine-human-

81. Ed Payne, "Transgender first-grader wins the right to use girls' restroom," CNN.com, 12/1/15, accessed 7/20/13, http://www.cnn.com/2013/06/24/us/colorado-transgender-girl-school/index.html

82. Deena Winter, "Nebraska school suggests teachers avoid calling students boys or girls to be 'gender inclusive,'" Nebraska Watchdog.org, 10/2/14, accessed 1/16/16, http://watchdog.org/174768/gender-inclusive/

83. John McKellar, "Homosexuals Against Pride Extremism," Catholic-legate.com, 3/15/08, accessed 6/2/16, http://www.catholic-legate.com/homosexual-against-pride-extremism/

84. Alana Horowitz, "Pope Francis 'Shocked' By Gay Adoption Bill: Report," Huffingtonpost.com, 12/29/13, accessed 1/8/16, http://www.huffingtonpost.com/2013/12/29/pope-francis-gay-adoption_n_4516304.html

85. Cavan Sieczkowski, "Pope Francis Against Gay Marriage, Gay Adoption," Huffingtonpost.com, 3/13/13, accessed 1/8/16, http://www.huffingtonpost.com/2013/03/13/pope-francis-gay-marriage-anti_n_2869221.html

86. Ravi Zacharias, "Tradegy at Newtown," 12/18/12. Accessed 4/10/16, http://www.malankaraworld.com/library/Reading/Suffering/Suffering_Tragedy-At-Newtown-RZ.htm

87. Kirsten Powers, "Philadelphia abortion clinic horror: We've forgotten what belongs on Page One," USAToday.com, 4/11/13, accessed 1/8/16, http://www.usatoday.com/story/opinion/2013/04/10/philadelphia-abortion-clinic-horror-column/2072577/

88. Grand Jury Report Against Kermit Gosnell, 2011, accessed 6/2/16, www.phila.gov/districtattorney/pdfs/grandjurywomensmedical.pdf

89. Ibid.

90. Ibid.

91. "Surgical Abortion - Second Trimester Abortion," CherryHillWomensCenter.com, accessed 1/8/16, http://www.cherryhillwomenscenter.com/abortion-care/2nd-trimester-abortion/

92. "Warning:Smoking during pregnancy can harm your baby," FDA.gov, 4/13, accessed 1/15/16 http://www.fda.gov/TobaccoProducts/Labeling/ucm231357.htm

93. "Alcoholic Beverage Labeling Act," Wikipedia, accessed 1/8/16, http://en.wikipedia.org/wiki/Alcoholic_Beverage_Labeling_Act

94. "Women," Cornell University, Deathpenaltyworldwide.org, accessed 1/8/16, http://www.deathpenaltyworldwide.org/women.cfm

95. Francis A. Schaffer and C. Everett Koop, *Whatever Happened to the Human Race?* Crossway Books, Wheaton, Illinois, 1979.

96. "Pope Francis denounces abortion as part of the 'throwaway culture,'" Torontocatholicwitness.com, accessed 1/8/16, http://torontocatholicwitness.blogspot.com/2014/01/pope-francis-denounces-abortion-as-part.html

97. Monica Migliorino Miller, *Abandoned: The Untold Story of the Abortion Wars*, Saint Benedict Press, Charlotte, North Carolina, 2012.

98. Saint Augustine of Hippo (354-430 AD), "Our Heart is Restless Until it Rest in You" from *Confessions,* Book 1, Chapter 1, piercedhearts.org, accessed 1/8/16, http://www.piercedhearts.org/theology_heart/teaching_saints/hearts_restless_st_augustine.htm

99. Ron Rhodes, "Manuscript Support for the Bible's Reliability," Reasoning From Scripture Ministries, Earthlink.net, accessed 1/17/16, http://home.earthlink.net/~ronrhodes/Manuscript.html

100. "What does it mean when the Bible says the kingdom of God is within you?" Let Us Reason Ministries, accessed 1/8/16, http://www.letusreason.org/Biblexp47.htm

101. Billy Hallowell, "Top 5 Moments From Bill O'Reilly's 'Killing Jesus' Interview With '60 Minutes,'" The Blaze, 9/30/13, accessed 1/8/16, http://www.theblaze.com/stories/2013/09/30/top-5-moments-from-bill-oreillys-killing-jesus-interview-with-60-minutes/

102. "Chelyabinsk meteor," Wikipedia, accessed 1/8/16, http://en.wikipedia.org/wiki/Chelyabinsk_meteor

103. "Asteroid 'narrowly' misses Earth on day meteorite hits Russia," The Guardian, accessed 1/8/16, http://www.theguardian.com/science/video/2013/feb/16/asteroid-misses-earth-video

104. "Meteors, Asteroids & Now This: Fireball Seen Streaking Across the San Francisco Sky," The Blaze, accessed 1/8/16, http://www.theblaze.com/stories/2013/02/16/meteors-asteroids-now-this-fireball-seen-streaking-across-the-san-francisco-sky/

105. "Did You See the Fireball Light Up the Night Sky Over South Florida?" The Blaze, accessed 1/8/16, http://www.theblaze.com/stories/2013/02/18/did-you-see-the-fireball-light-up-the-night-sky-over-south-florida/

106. "Moral Decline," Conservapedia.com, accessed 1/8/16, http://www.conservapedia.com/Moral_decline

Thank you for reading *Broken Land.* If the message of this book resonates with you, I would appreciate your taking a moment to write a review on Amazon, as well as on other sites like Barnes and Noble, Christian Book, etc. If I get 50 reviews on Amazon, then when a customer buys a similar book, Amazon will say, "Customers who bought this item also bought..." and will include *Broken Land* in the list.

If you send a link to your review (just copy and paste the address from the browser) to me or my publisher (gailfkoop@aol.com or olivepressbooks@gmail.com), we would like to thank you with some bonus material and a special gift. Please include your mailing address to receive the gift.

I am grateful to be able to partner with you to help others realize that only God can heal our broken land.

– Gail Koop

BROKEN LAND

is available at:

olivepresspublisher.com

amazon.com

barnesandnoble.com

christianbook.com

deepershopping.com

and other online stores

Store managers:

Order wholesale through:

Ingram Book Company or

Spring Arbor

or by emailing:

olivepressbooks@gmail.com

Author's email and website:

gailfkoop@aol.com

www.framedbytheword.com